fifty GREAT YEARS
1897 - 1947

THROUGH THE EYES OF THE
EVENING CHRONICLE

NARRATIVE (except signed articles) written by

HENRY J. BRADLEY

ILLUSTRATION and MONTAGES

by WILFRID LYTH

DRAWINGS in signed articles by

WALTER CRAWFORD JONES

REPUBLISHED BY

'Memories'

Castlefield Publications,
Dawson Street,
Manchester M3 4JZ

ISBN 1 899181 30 X

Published by: "Memories"
                  Castlefield Publication
                  Dawson Street
                  Manchester

First published in 1947
Original Title "Fifty Great Years"

Prepared by: *liff Hayes*

Distributed by: **N.P.S.**
                  28 Bedford Road
                  Firswood
                  Manchester

                  tel: **0161 862 9399**

Printed by: **MFP Design & Print**

                  tel: **0161 864 4540**

ORIGINAL ACKNOWLEDGEMENT

THE EDITOR wishes to acknowledge valuable assistance given by the Physical Society (for permission to reproduce the picture of Lord Rutherford and Dr. Geiger), The Manchester Museum and Mr. R. U. Sayce, The Henry Watson Music Library and Mr. John F. Russell, The Manchester Geographical Society, The British Broadcasting Corporation, Belle Vue (Manchester) Ltd., Messrs. George Whittaker and Sons, Stalybridge (for picture of Jack Judge, and details of the origin of " Tipperary " from their booklet, *Laycock, Jack Judge and J. C. Prince*), Messrs. Foulsham and Banfield (for photographs of " Hindle Wakes " and Miss Lily Elsie), St. James's Ward Conservative Club, Oldham, The Mayor and Corporation of Blackpool, Mr. A. Eden, Mr. A. Hunter and Mr. F. Yates (for pictures of old Blackpool), Mr. W. A. Hewitson, Mr. H. C. Lomax, Mr. T. Roberts, Mr. M. C. Grimley, Mr. P. W. Bury, Mr. Victor Smythe, Mr. J. C. Robertson, Mr. P. J. Conroy, Mr. H. Hindle, Mr. R. Walker, Mr. E. P. Gaul, and Miss D. Howard.

ORIGINAL TITLE PAGE

1897 — FIFTY GREAT YEARS — 1947

COMPILED AND EDITED BY

"DENYS"

OF "THROUGH A NORTHERN WINDOW"

PRODUCED TO MARK THE

GOLDEN JUBILEE

OF THE

Evening Chronicle

FIRST PUBLISHED MAY 10, 1897

THIS EDITION PUBLISHED BY

'Memories'

Introduction

Almost 100 years ago on May 10th 1897 a new newspaper hit the streets. It was the "Manchester Chronicle" and it became a great success. After 50 years of publishing it produced a 'look back' and it is that book which is reproduced here.

The Chronicle was informative, gossipy and well-written newspaper, always there with the latest news and views. This shows in their "Fifty Great Years" a book which captures every major event as it was reflected in the North.

Some five years ago Tony Gibb of Gibbs Book Shop in Charlotte Street Manchester, introduced me to the book and I have read and re-read it. I have found it a wonderful source of information for the radio spots and local history talks I give. It has helped me understand the Boer War and why the people of Lancashire did not take it seriously at first. The pictures are different and personal; Churchill in Oldham; the Music Hall stars of the Edwardian era; stars of the sporting world and Manchester at war. I have been selfish enough to keep the book for myself, but now I think it deserves to be shared with anyone interested in the history of the North West and Manchester.

Find out about Jack Judge and Tipperary, the 'Arsenic in the Beer' scandal, the Suffragettes and the characters of the past.

Anyone who wants to know more about the world of our parents and grandparents must read . . .

FIFTY GREAT YEARS
1897-1947

FIFTY GREAT YEARS are here under review. Fifty great years for that important region of England centred on Manchester —and for the EVENING CHRONICLE.

For this period the EVENING CHRONICLE has sought daily truly and comprehensively to mirror the rich and varied activities of a mighty city and its environs.

The local newspaper can play a great part in the life of a community, and I have no hesitation in saying that under the control of directors at the very centre of production the EVENING CHRONICLE has played its part fully in the past. It is my aim, as Chairman of Kemsley Newspapers, that this bond shall be further strengthened in the years to come.

This book is offered as a worthy record of the first fifty years, and a pledge for the future.

Kemsley

VISCOUNT KEMSLEY'S MESSAGE

As it was . . . . .

By James Agate

I HAVE no objective view of Manchester. In '97 I was twenty, and if I am to tell readers of the EVENING CHRONICLE what at that age I thought about my native city—actually I was born in Salford—I must have recourse to an inventory of my sensations from the days when I was ousted from my perambulator by the brother next in age. I still have in my nostrils the pungent odour of decaying leaves on the wet flag-stones of the Seedley Road.

Now comes the musty smell of the yellow cabs belonging, if I remember correctly, to the Manchester Carriage and Tramways Company. (I cannot at this date hope to be entirely accurate in the matter of names.) Yellow, noisy, tyreless, commodious vehicles, rejoicing interiorly in Sitwellian sumptuosity of fading red velvet. The Company had its headquarters at what still seems to me to be a remarkable confluence of thoroughfares. There is the road which leads from Pendleton to Manchester proper, passing Peel Park, that museum which I never saw anybody leave or enter, the statue of that prig who maintained that his riches consisted in the fewness of his wants, and that desolate, dank, peninsula of nothingness almost entirely surrounded by the river Irwell. The road which was to become the Eccles Old Road where the " nice " people lived and houses were painted in the classiest shades of yellow ochre and magenta. The road leading to Irlams-o'-th'-Height, where collieries abounded and the working classes presumably did whatever it befits working classes to do. A dreadful little street down by St. Thomas's Church, a street in which I never set foot. The Seedley Road where we lived, and not to be confused with the Lower Seedley Road, where music-masters huggered and the letters of lodgings muggered. Behind was the limbo of Ellor Street, where everybody fried fish, and down which Father, Mother, and four sons processed to Sunday Chapel and were laughed at and bethumbed by rude, dirty little boys. The chapel caretaker was far uglier and more terrifying than Quilp; he was the only man I have ever known with hair on the palms of his hands.

I remember the shops to which, as a small boy, I accompanied my mother. The grocer at the corner was called Knowles. The greengrocer next door was Hyde—I remember that it was outside the greengrocer's

that a sturdy young ruffian blacked my eye after opining that I was ridiculously dressed. (I was!) The shoemaker was called Mason. He was very Scotch, and had a way of passing his thumb over the toe of the most uncomfortable shoe with so many encomiums on the quality of the leather that you forgot about the fit. The chemist was called Harrop, and nothing would have shaken my allegiance in favour of a newcomer called Blore, but the fact that Mr. Blore dealt in photographic requisites and Mr. Harrop didn't. Butcher, baker and draper were respectively named Lancaster, Worsley, and Pearson, while the man who kept the post office, whose name I forget, dealt in a cluttersome sort of way in hay and straw. There was one old lady who lived entirely by the sale of Berlin wool, and another who made tarts which you were not allowed to buy unless she liked the look of you.

I PASS over the years I spent at the hideously-housed Manchester Grammar School, where I imbibed a lot of learning and no corporate spirit, whereas at Giggleswick I learned nothing except how to behave. At eighteen I was a prefect and wore a mortar-board and hated it, and at my final prize-giving gave a magnificent performance in the Free Trade Hall of Don Diègue in Corneille's " Le Cid." From '95 to '97 I worked in my father's mill, at Nelson, the idea being that a man who was to spend his life selling cotton goods should know how they are made. Every morning I caught the 8-33, missing the train on two occasions only and taking the 9-33. On each occasion, once soon after leaving Pendleton, and once just approaching Burnley, a man came from behind a bridge and laid his head on the rails.

I NOW come to Salford's trams which played a great part in my life. They were horse-drawn, and at the end of a journey the pair of willing slaves had to be unhitched and re-yoked at the other end. This persisted until the day came when some bright spirit had the notion of turning the car round on its own axis. How can trams have played so great a part in my life? Simply that I went to work at my father's Manchester office twice a day, returning home for lunch. Six journeys of 20 minutes each amounts to two hours, and it is to the useful employment of those two hours over a period of years that I owe that stock of reading which stands me in good stead today. Manchester in those days was a capital and had the atmosphere of a capital. It had the best newspaper in the world, a paper whose supremacy nothing, as far as I am concerned, has been able to shake. In the *Manchester Guardian* we read what was doing in the theatres of London, and, what is more, we realized that these doings still awaited the seal of Manchester's approval. I have a little book of republished theatre criticisms of the period which says : " The line was taken that a city such as Manchester could claim the application of the strictest standards, just as if it were London or Paris." Beardsley might write of :

> . . . *réclame and recall,*
> *Paris and St. Petersburg, Vienna and*
> *St. James's Hall.*

We in Manchester talked of :

> . . . *réclame and recall,*
> *Paris and St. Petersburg, Vienna and the*
> *Free Trade Hall.*

I shall come to the Hallé concerts later. In those days the Royal and the Princes were theatres in being. The first, uphol-stered in

red and scorning frivolity, saw the regular visits of Irving, Benson, Alexander, Tree. The Princes was a smiling affair of light blue with dainty lace antimacassars and gold everywhere. Here we saw Evie Green, Gertie Millar, Lily Elsie and all the stars of the musical comedy world. Round about this period we had astonishing and cometary visitations—Bernhardt in *La Tosca, Fédora* and *La Dame aux Camélias.* Coquelin in *Cyrano de Bergerac* and *Le Bourgeois Gentilhomme.* Elizabeth Robins in *The Master Builder.* Charles Charrington and Janet Achurch in *A Doll's House* and *Candida.* Mrs. Patrick Campbell and George Alexander in *The Second Mrs. Tanqueray.* Perhaps I may be permitted a story here, though it rightly belongs to a period 10 years later when I was doing 'prentice work as dramatic critic on the *Manchester Guardian.* Alexander in some drawing-room comedy had said to his blackmailer: "Sir, your conduct is despicable!" And next morning I pointed out that the accent should be on the first and not the second syllable. Once again during the week I went to see the play, and again Alexander brought his fist down on the table. But this time he said: "Sir, your conduct is *dastardly!*"

WHAT fun at Christmas time these two theatres, the Royal and the Princes, provided! The pantomimes at the Royal had about them that quality which Coleridge calls working poetry. They were compact of glamour, solid, substantial and thick. You were assured before you went of fun Faster and Furiouser than Ever Before. There you could see the unforgettable Maggie Duggan

and George Robey at his unequalled best. And there I did in fact see the début of George Graves. The pantomimes at the Princes, supervised by Robert Courtneidge, were of a different order. Charm and not sensation was their note, and the scenery of Conrad Tritschler set one a-tingle with delight. I was so much struck with the exquisite colour-scheme of a ballet, palest primrose deepening to ripest orange, that I wrote an article about it and sent it to the *Daily Dispatch.* Which paper next morning set my foot on the first rung of dramatic criticism.

THIS is perhaps the place to confess that out of my weekly wages of two pounds I spent 10 shillings on piano lessons given by a music master at Didsbury. The point is that in my day young people had to account for their evening movements, and I was forbidden the music hall. Now the Manchester Palace of Variety lay half-way between Didsbury and Pendleton and, my music master conniving, I was able to cut my lesson in those weeks in which Marie Lloyd and Vesta Tilley appeared at the Palace. I kept up this deception for ten years. The only other time I played truant, as it were, was in the summer when there was some particularly exciting match at Old Trafford. Great days of Manchester cricket! Hornby running out Barlow, and Barlow pretending to like it. Archie MacLaren, Neville Cardus's "noblest Roman," who put more grandeur into the compiling of a duck than any other batsman into a century. Albert Ward, who batted in the way that some authors write dull, impeccable prose, J. T. Tyldesley, uncannily combining impudence with certainty. Johnny

Briggs delivering the ball a yard behind the crease and making his extraordinary stroke over coverpoint's head. The interminable Lancashire tail, and the clouds massing over the Stretford end. I was never afraid of being caught playing truant after the day I caught my father playing truant, too.

I SUPPOSE Manchester is a plain city? I would rather say that she is like a beauty who does not know how to dress. But in '97 it did not occur to me to ask the question. Manchester was Manchester and didn't pretend to be Oxford or Edinburgh. And whatever Manchester did was, in my eyes, right. There was an Art Gallery which we were encouraged to visit, and where we gazed at Ford Madox Brown's " Work " and felt ourselves every inch the perfect pre-Raphaelite.

There was Mudie's, the lending library, where I was sent to change the books, and where my brother Edward and I laid out sevenpence-halfpenny weekly—or was it tenpence? —till we had acquired the complete Calmann Lévy edition of Balzac, which we then had bound in stylish buckram. The fifty volumes are within two yards of my desk today. There

was John Mark, the grocer, where we shopped whenever there was to be a party. There was Parker's, which sold the best coffee and made the best cakes I have ever tasted. " Excuse me, miss," said a seven-year-old, later on to be President of the Manchester Society of Architects, and eyeing a plate of delicious confectionery, " do you charge by time? " Everything that was sold in Manchester was " good," in the sense that Mrs. Baines's furniture in the Arnold Bennett novel was " good." The watch you bought at Ollivant and Botsford's, in 1897, is keeping correct time today; the trunk with which Finnigan's equipped the schoolboy stands up to whatever old age requires of it. (I am not advertising these firms any more than a

traveller recording his impressions of Switzerland can be said to advertise Mont Blanc.) I remember Satterfield's, where every Christmas I bought my mother a pair of six-button, French, suède gloves costing four shillings and sixpence, or nine weeks' pocket money. I just don't believe that such gloves are being made today. The shop at which my parents bought me my first boy's suit was called Macbeth's, and I had some notion that the proprietor was a descendant, say a great-grandson, of Shakespeare's character. Then there was Kendal Milne's, the great drapery emporium. Now '97 was the very heyday of the Kendals, Mrs. Kendal being to the theatre what Queen Victoria was to the Empire. In a childish, Alice-in-Wonderland sort of way, some of the glory of the name transferred itself in my mind to a firm with which the actress had nothing to do. To this day to say the words"Kendal Milne" in my hearing is exactly as though somebody had mentioned the British Empire to Rudyard Kipling.

THE Hallé concerts? I have left these to the last because they are the first in my mind. I was taken to them at the age of seven, and listened to many an interminable oratorio with feet not reaching to the floor. Hallé, grave and conscientious. (My dates here are something elastic.) Norman Neruda, as ugly as any woman might reasonably expect to be, but with her exquisite bowing arm and perfect mastery of the Mendelssohn concerto ; it was an invariable rule that whenever she came on to the platform the audience should rise to its feet. Carreño giving the first Manchester performance of the Tchaikovsky concerto. Paderewski, Pachmann, d'Albert, Rosenthal, Busoni, Joachim, Sarasate, Ysaye. All the world's greatest singers. The best cast that the " Messiah " ever had—Lloyd, Santley, Albani, Crossley. Richter conducting the first Manchester performance of

Sunny afternoon in Piccadilly, Manchester, 50 years ago. Practically all the buildings seen on the left side of the picture have been reconstructed. The open-topped horse trams were scrapped in 1901

Tchaikovsky's *Pathétique* and laying down his bâton in the second movement, leaving the orchestra to itself. Richter giving Manchester its first Symphonic Poem—Strauss's *Don Juan*. And next morning a notice of the concert equal to anything penned in London, Paris, Berlin.

ALL the Manchester of my youth was spent under the wing of, let me reiterate, the greatest newspaper in the world. But since it is possible that a guest at one of Jupiter's parties, bidden to take Minerva

R. H. Wilson, Hallé Chorus Master in the palmiest days of oratorio

in to dinner, might ask for a little relief on the left, so one welcomed the advent of the MANCHESTER EVENING CHRONICLE. The effect of the *Guardian* was to make one feel that the previous day had been one of grave moral questioning and serious responsibility at home and abroad. The CHRONICLE gave one the impression that the day one had just lived through had been full of exciting and, on the whole, jolly happenings. One would be serious again in the morning. But for the moment it seemed that, on the whole, the world was fun.

Edward Lloyd created the tenor parts in many famous oratorios

. . . . in the beginning

By T. Thompson

THERE are two sharply defined schools of thought about the nineties. There are those who swear that Fanny by Gaslight could not have helped being naughty, times being what they were, and the other blood-group who fancy Victoria's reign as steaming with prudery and cluttered up with anti-macassars and aspidistras. They cannot both be right, but both are entitled to their say. What was it like in the nineties in Lancashire ?

I was there and I remember it well as a conglomeration of money-making, poverty, sancti-mony, illiteracy, heroism and illusion. Above all individuality. Every mean street was as rich in characters as a Dickens novel. You never knew what they would do next and they were as full of robust comedy as Falstaff or Sancho Panza. They worked hard, they drank hard, they fought hard, they roared with laughter in Rabelaisan jest, and despite or because of their poverty they were mainly Tories.

My own grandmother who first went to work at the age of five and was still at it when turned seventy, used to read Tory speeches by candle light and would most certainly have turned her back on Gladstone to spit on the floor had she had the misfortune to meet him. Yet she was a grand woman and could face anything without blinking her eyes.

WALTER C JONES

THEY would have laughed if they could have heard our present chatter about austerity. They could not have distinguished it from luxury. The cottage in which I was born was like all the others in the street and the street was like all the others in the district. It had two tiny rooms downstairs and two up. There was a back door which opened directly on the back street and there was no yard. Some cottages were indeed " back to back " and had only one door. I doubt if one of them was carpeted, but the flagged floors were scrupulously clean and sprinkled with sand. It was often said that one could eat off the floors they were so clean, but my grandmother held that it was better to see a few grease spots in evidence of good eating. The hearthstone was pipe-clayed and patted with a damp floor-cloth to make a primitive pattern.

Sanitary arrangements were unspeakable. Five cottages joined at a pail closet and behind this was a wet open midden where all sorts of refuse was thrown. In summer flies had a real picnic. There was not a fixed bath in the street and Friday night was a steamy affair when the big pan was put on the fire and kept going until the whole household was more or less bodily clean. Then the zinc bath was wiped round, removed from front of the fire, and hung in the kitchen until next week.

A GOOD COOK was one who could make a meal out of an old towel. The broth pan was a great standby and into it went almost anything that could be obtained. A "ham pestil," some pearl barley, "Pot herbs," which meant celery tops, leek trimmings, and vegetable debris which could be bought for a few coppers at the greengrocers, suet dumplings, "block ornaments" or bits of meat collected by the butcher to sell cheaply, all went into the pan to make a savoury mess which was cheap, filling and wholesome. A good potato pie also made a good meal.

It must be said that in prosperous times the family was well fed with plain wholesome food, though a joint was seldom seen. Bread was baked at home, kneaded with potato water and brewer's yeast. Almost every public house brewed its own beer and was open all day from six in the morning until the last customer decided to go home at night. It was considered no shame to go with a jug for the supper beer for the last meal of the day. One good thing could be said for the times. There were few inhibitions.

All bedrooms were white-washed, mainly done by the man of the house. The kitchen, too, was white-washed and only the living room was papered crudely. The gaspipe hung starkly from the ceiling and illumination was by a naked gas flame. Candles were used in bedrooms.

At Christmas the gaspipe was decorated with twisted and

crimped, coloured tissue japer. Sprigs of holly and mistletoe were tucked across the pictures on the wall and garish "mottoes" were also tacked upon the wall wishing "A Merry Christmas" or wondering "What is Home without a Mother?" What indeed?

The children hung their stockings up as now. I usually managed to get an apple, an orange, and a sugar pig with a red worsted tail, sometimes covered with cinders as a crude practical joke.

The toffee shops gave Christmas boxes of boiled sweets and the grocers picture calendars. A local tripe works manager heated pennies on a shovel and tossed them over the gate to watch the children burn their fingers as they scrambled for the untold wealth. Fathers got drunk and were either put to bed, or, if capable kicked the family out of doors. It was indeed the festive season.

A BIG family was then a good investment. As soon as ready the youngsters were put into the cotton mills, then the main source of employment. Education was perfunctory. There were School Board officers whose duty it was to see that children went to school. But the system was by no means efficient and provided the child kept out of their way it could "wag it" with something like impunity.

Even if it did go to school the better scholar it could prove to be the easier it could escape. It was possible then to pass what

The Victorian stone cottage, typical of the Lancashire mill towns, in which T. Thompson was born at Bury

Deerstalkers and knickerbockers have vanished since these holidaymakers were photographed at Llandudno in the year of Queen Victoria's Diamond Jubilee. But one thing remains unchanged — the traditional Punch and Judy show

was known as a "labour examination," which allowed it to leave school earlier and go to work. It was held then that brains could be better used outside school than in, and thus the scholar was taught to swim by the simple expedient of throwing it in the water. The present process of educating the brilliant scholar on and on to the university, safe job and oblivion did not obtain.

The system worked well in many cases. There were some big successes, some Jimmy Whites, and many total wrecks. Many, including myself, went "half-time" in the mills, attending school one half-day and working the other. We went full-time working at 12.

We dressed for the job. An iron moulder could be recognized by the mole-skin trousers he wore to keep the sparks from his legs. The tackler by his overalls, and the weaver by her clogs and shawl. There was no indignity felt about this.

The age of the female was denoted by the change in dress. Her hair was "put up"

when about 19 and her frocks were lengthened in stages until legs ceased entirely to be worn except on very windy days. Both women and men were old at 50.

Photographs of the dress of the period are laughed at now, just as photographs of the present day will be laughed at 50 years hence. Human dress has always been preposterous and always will be. The nudist has logic on his side.

When all the members of a big family were working

there would be real prosperity, and the family usually "flitted" to a house with a "lobby" and a parlour. Here was real distinction, only to be enhanced by the purchase of a piano. The parlour was seldom used until one or other of the family began courting and was allowed occasional solitude in its stuffy atmosphere.

With prosperity began a social change and a black-coated element began to spring from the lower reaches of the family. The older children would work with their hands to allow the younger element to exercise their brains. It was rough on the older ones, but the family was proud to include a teacher or an office worker in its ranks. The piano began to be tuned and even played.

THE cotton mill was neither a Paradise nor an El Dorado in those days, and the industry is now paying for its shortcomings in those earlier times. The older generation have long memories. The light industries had not yet arrived to compete for labour and it was either work in the mills or clem. Sometimes it was work in the mills and also clem.

Occasionally, cotton crises arrived—because somebody across the sea made a determined bid to "corner" cotton, or because of some glut in the market. There was then no unemployment insurance. The mills were closed and the pawnshops flourished. I have fed myself in the soup kitchens provided to keep the cotton workers alive, and I remember Wilson Barrett, the actor, being so moved by the privations of the cotton workers that he sent hampers of loaves to my home town.

They were grim days. Yet the chief characteristic of that time was its seeming solidity. The mill chimneys seemed as permanent as the pyramids. Cotton and Lancashire seemed to be one and indivisible.

SUDDENLY Lancashire woke up to the fact that it was extremely illiterate and half educated. A passion for education sprang up amongst young and old. It ought to be remembered, but is not, that the Co-operative Movement was the great pioneer in this urge for adult and technical education.

The local Co-operative Society in almost every Lancashire town began evening classes for ordinary and technical education. In my home town they were attended by grown-up people and especially by soldiers from the local barracks. They were the only continuation and technical classes, and persisted until the local authorities took them over.

Libraries were also formed in connection with Sunday schools and it was through one of these that I began to read Dickens, Thackeray, and other classics of the time. They did a grand job just when it was most needed. I raise my hat to those sturdy pioneers.

IT was the age of "cards." Every Lancashire town had

The girls they flirted with at Blackpool in the Nineties. A costume could be bought for half-a-guinea, a braided cape for 5s. 11d. Blouses cost as little as 1s. 0½d., and shoes 2s. 11d. to 5s. 6d. It was possible to look pretty for a pound

one or more and they were almost worshipped by everybody except their creditors. They made money ruthlessly and spent it with equal exuberance. They were racily costumed, wearing flowered silk waistcoats, sported a carnation buttonhole and a grey box hat.

They spreed and gambled with their own and other people's money. Up they went like a rocket and down they came like the stick. They were generous and generally bawdy. Good to look at and bad to live with. Their wives were down-trodden and apprehensive and their mistresses arrogant and resplendent.

They became a legend in their towns and strange tales were fathered upon them whether true or otherwise. It was a time when audacity could easily live on simplicity and ignorance, and they made full use of their opportunities. The best that could be said of them was that they were at least picturesque in a drab period.

WERE there then no fun and games? Most certainly there were. It is difficult to think that there was a time when there were no cinemas, no motor cars, no electricity, no gramophones or any provided entertainment, except theatres, concerts, and penny readings. But this meant that folks had to make their own fun and this they did with great gusto and sometimes vulgarity.

There was whippet racing, Lancashire wrestling (almost all-in), boxing, " peggy " playing, running, dancing, singing, a fair amount of hole in the corner cock-fighting (I remember raids in the centre of the town), street games, and the usual Sunday School parties. Among the very poor holidays were not always welcomed as they meant the loss of a wage. The blessing of a holiday with pay had not yet arrived.

THE annual holiday was four days about August. Only the aristocrats of industry had a week. What a holiday it was ! We went to Blackpool on the Saturday and arrived there before breakfast and we came home on Tuesday to arrive about midnight or after.

There was a walk on the prom before breakfast every day we were there, with lashings of rum and coffee and oysters. Then we danced on the pier all the morning, took a landau in the afternoon and danced inside all the evening.

We philandered with the opposite sex from other towns, corresponded with them for about three weeks and then forgot them entirely. We slept three in a bed and four beds in the room. It was intensive jollification and it took a whole year to recover from the resulting debility.

THOSE were the days ! My friend Wilfred Pickles tells me that to make a success of his " Have a Go " programmes he must seek out the primitive Lancastrian or Northerner to achieve success. They alone have the character and humour necessary. The more education they have imbibed the duller they seem to be.

There would seem to be a problem for the educationalists here. How to enlighten the native and at the same time retain his natural salt and savour. As Hamlet said, " That is the question." Indisputably we are far better off materially and mentally than ever before. Or would be, but for war.

War ! In those early days a shadow no bigger than a man's hand. Now a thunder cloud that shuts out the sun and puts fear into our hearts. Then we kept our wars at a respectable distance. Now they tumble about our ears. They shout at us from stage and screen, and broadcasting brings them to our homes.

Amidst all the primitive discomforts of the nineties there was less forboding than now when there is no such thing as distance, and folly is more explosive. These are the perplexities of the days in which we now live. Do we laugh or do we weep ? I am all for laughter, endeavour, and infinite patience.

Mr. T. Thompson, the author

Enter the Narrator

On the afternoon of May 10th, 1897, there was a crisis among the newsboys at Mr. Faulkner's shop in Broughton Road, Salford. The newsagent, surrounded by stacks of papers, offered the boys a new one — THE MANCHESTER EVENING CHRONICLE. The lads looked at each other uncertainly. A new paper was a gamble with the unknown; it might be left on their hands. Suddenly one boy ran forward and said: " I'll take two dozen "—and dashed away. " I wish I'd taken ten dozen," he said an hour later, thinking of the extra pennies that would have been his.

What was happening in Broughton Road was being repeated in hundreds of newsagents shops all over Manchester, Lancashire and Cheshire. By nightfall the North had looked at the new paper and liked it so well that it had bought 169,000 copies.

Let us turn back 200,000 pages and look at the infant of 1897. It was a fine child, six pages the first night and eight thereafter. The days were to come when its waistband had to be widened to take in 16, 20 and even 24 pages. But 50 years ago an eight-page evening paper was a novelty. The usual size was four or six.

To newspaper readers of 1947 the type of that first issue looks small and solid. Headlines never expanded beyond one column and, indeed, just about the only thing that has not changed in 50 years is the method of setting the cricket scores. In one way, however, the CHRONICLE was ahead of most of its contemporary competitors. It carried six illustrations in its first issue, including a fashion sketch and a cartoon of Kruger.

Foreign news was brief. In those days even imperialists were mostly " Little Englanders " in the sense that they did not know a great deal about affairs overseas. In compensation Lancashire was vividly concerned with its own affairs. It was the home of a million fewer people then it is to-day and the distribution of population and industry was different. Blackpool, for instance, was still a small town of 35,000 people and Trafford Park, which now employs 50,000 workers, was still an expanse of grassy fields upon which, the EVENING CHRONICLE announced, preparations were being made to hold the Royal Agricultural Show.

Wages were low, but so were prices. Our first day's advertisements show that Old Gold cigarettes could be bought at 10 for 3d., best coal was 9d. a cwt., a duck cost 1s. 9d., a 40-piece china tea-set 12s. 6d. Above all it was possible to rent a tolerable house for as low as 4s. a week.

600 TURKEYS TO BE SOLD AT 4d., 5d., and 6d. PER LB.,

A dozen theatres advertised in our first issue. George Robey was announced at the Comedy, and our first theatrical picture was of Albert Chevalier. The first book noticed was Kipling's " Captains Courageous."

The cotton trade was prosperous, and the belief that British goods were best reigned supreme. Symptomatic was a testimonial from an overseas customer to the Manchester firm of John Noble printed in No. 1 of the EVENING CHRONICLE. She told how a costume had been sent by a boat which sank. The costume was salvaged and declared to be " little damaged."

The founder of the EVENING CHRONICLE was Edward Hulton who, in 1897, was an energetic, bearded man of 59. He was born near Withy Grove, whose name he was to make known throughout Britain, and started life without advantages. " I had to rely on my own resources," he said. In 1871, with the aid of E. O. Bleackley, of Prestwich, he started *The Prophetic Bell*, published in Spear Street. Soon a move was made to Withy Grove and there, in quick succession, Hulton founded *The Sporting Chronicle* and the *Athletic News*. He was the first newspaper man to appreciate that a new public interested in athletics, cycling and games of all kinds was growing up.

Queen Victoria. A Jubilee portrait

But his interests and ambitions ranged far outside sport, as he proved when he founded the *Sunday Chronicle* in 1885 and, 12 years later, the EVENING CHRONICLE. Success brought fortune, but Hulton had no pride of living, and his own career gave him shrewd, first-hand knowledge and understanding of the working man, especially the Conservative working man, whose stronghold Lancashire then was.

This type distrusted the Liberal magnates; was attracted by Disraeli's dream of Tory Democracy and, at some points, stood to the left of the Radicals of the day. Hulton's own opinions ran on parallel lines. When the engineers struck in July, 1897, for the eight-hour day the infant EVENING CHRONICLE'S first comment on the dispute hinged on William Mather's declaration that the shorter day had been beneficial in his own works.

Nelson's flagship, the *Foudroyant*, wrecked on Blackpool sands, June, 1897

THE new evening paper had plenty of vivid local news to report in its first few weeks. In June, 1897, came the Diamond Jubilee on which Manchester Corporation spent £10,000. Then the Foudroyant, the 80-gun "wooden wall" in which Nelson sailed to meet Lady Hamilton in Naples, was wrecked in a storm at Blackpool. As soon as the gale dropped "an advertisement fiend" waded out and pasted on the wreck "advice to the public to take certain pills." A few days later there was further excitement at Blackpool. The top platform of the new Tower was discovered to be ablaze.

The great sensation of the summer was the suicide of Barney Barnato, most fantastic of Rand millionaires. Another millionaire bubble burst a few months later when Derbyshire-bred E. T. Hooley went bankrupt, owing £1,500,000. About the same time the EVENING CHRONICLE had news of Jabez Balfour, the one-time White Hope of Nonconformity and ex-candidate for Burnley, whose Liberator frauds cost a host of investors £7,000,000. He was now in gaol and working in the quarries. "Clogs to clogs in three generations" ran the Lancashire adage, but these men accomplished the journey in a decade or so ! Manchester's own contribution to the melodrama of the time was acted unrehearsed, on July 6th, 1898. In the County Court, Judge Parry cancelled the certificates of two bailiffs. One of them, William Taylor, a wild, white-bearded figure sprang to his feet, drew a revolver, and fired three shots at point blank range. The judge, wounded in the chin and throat, sank back in his chair, " a ghastly spectacle with blood streaming down his face and neck."

Cries of " Murder ! " ran round the court, but Parry recovered to enjoy a long career as both judge and author.

THE background to such excitements was solid and reassuring ; Lancashire people were rising in the scale of prosperity. There was much money and much enterprise in the county, not only for business but for pleasure, amenity and the arts.

Visible signs of this were, at one extreme, the new Tower at Blackpool and the still newer Big Wheel. At the other extreme were the building of the unsurpassed John Rylands Library and the bold stroke which brought Hans Richter to be conductor of the Hallé Orchestra. He, the world's greatest conductor, left Vienna to live in Lancashire.

"Lancashire," wrote Haslam Mills, " is only a county, but it has always given itself the airs of a continent." In the late Nineties and for some time after that was fair comment.

MR. GLADSTONE DEAD.

A PEACEFUL END.

DEEPLY AND UNIVERSALLY MOURNED.

THE CLOSE OF A LONG LIFE AND A GREAT CAREER.

The original Withy Grove office from which the *Evening Chronicle* was published from its birth until the 1920's

MANCHESTER
EVENING CHRONICLE

MONDAY, MAY 10, 1897.

PRICE ONE HALFPENNY.

No. 1.

THE CORPORATION OF THE
SCOTTISH PROVIDENT INSTITUTION.

HEAD OFFICE : No. 6 ST. ANDREW SQUARE, EDINBURGH.

THE ACCUMULATED FUNDS now exceed £10,000,000.

MANCHESTER BRANCH.

OFFICE—No. 11 ALBERT-SQUARE.

Champions of Plutocracy !

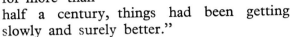

THE decent interval which now elapses between the death of an M.P. and the election of his successor, is a modern innovation. On a June Monday, in 1899, Mr. Robert Ascroft, Conservative M.P. for Oldham, died suddenly and before the week-end the struggle to fill his place was in full swing.

It was a queer election of tangled motives and forgotten controversies. It is remembered because it brought into politics, on opposing sides, two men whose names were first printed in the EVENING CHRONICLE as "Mr. W. L. S. Churchill and Mr. W. Runciman."

To 24-years'-old Winston Churchill Oldham seemed stranger than India's North-West Frontier or a cavalry charge at Omdurman. "There was," he noted, "no hotel in the town where one could hope to sleep . . . but there were many thousands of working-class homes where, for more than half a century, things had been getting slowly and surely better."

From one of these homes came Churchill's fellow Conservative candidate, Mr. Jim Mawdsley. "He was," said the future Prime Minister, "the most genuine specimen of the Tory working man I have ever come across. He boldly proclaimed admiration of Tory democracy and even of Tory Socialism."

THE mixture of "The Scion and the Socialist" did not upset the EVENING CHRONICLE, which argued that Oldham would do itself a bad turn if it did not return Jim Mawdsley, the one-time strike leader. It defended him stoutly against "the great Liberal organs who poke fun at his rugged grammar."

It was all in vain. As Churchill said : "My poor trade unionist friend and I would have had great difficulty in finding £500 between us, yet we were accused of representing the vested interests of society, while our opponents, who were good for a quarter of a million, claimed to champion the causes of the poor and needy."

On July 7 the workers of Oldham elected the wealthy Mr. Emmott and the equally rich Mr. Runciman as Liberal M.P.s. Churchill returned to London "with those feelings of deflation which a bottle of champagne or even soda water represents when it has been half-emptied and left uncorked for a night."

"Everyone threw the blame on me," he added. It was an overstatement. The EVENING CHRONICLE did not blame him. But it was much sorrier for Jim Mawdsley than for the young carpet-bagger.

Top : The young Churchill after his escape from the Boers

Left : With the Duke of Marlborough and the late Earl of Lytton, at Oldham, 1901

Mafeking—and All that

In the late summer of 1899 there was a change in the face of the EVENING CHRONICLE. For the first time, and for weeks on end, the main news headline ran across two columns. It was always the same—" The Transvaal Crisis."

So far as Lancashire was concerned, the drift to war was lighthearted. Big local news, like the opening of the John Rylands Library (October 6th), elbowed the crisis to the back of the paper, and on the day when the Boers invaded Natal we carried a portrait of Kruger, stating that it was his 74th birthday, and adding: "Many Happier Returns."

Then came the Boer victories, the gallantry of the Manchesters at Ladysmith, the famous sieges and the realization that we confronted a determined enemy

The tide of war turned in the spring of 1900. Kimberley was relieved and the EVENING CHRONICLE's sales soared to 341,000. March 1st was "A GREAT DAY." Ladysmith was freed—and 470,000 people bought the EVENING CHRONICLE.

On May 19th came news upon which "comment was superfluous." It was the relief of Mafeking. Manchester went nearly as crazy as

London, and our artists sketched street scenes in which false noses were worn beneath silk hats, ostrich feathers were crowned with Union Jacks, " Kruger's whiskers " were hoisted on poles and bands played everywhere. It was a very gay Saturday.

On the Monday the EVENING CHRONICLE leader began :

Are We An Emotional People ?
After a spree comes a sore head . . .

One man whose head was not made sore by war was a young Southport - born composer, Leslie Stuart. His " Soldiers of the Queen " was the hit of the year ; his " Floradora " drew packed houses, and with " The Lily of Laguna " he became the most popular song-writer of the day.

One story which thrilled Lancashire folk was the escape from the Boers of the young politician whom Oldham had rejected the previous year.

Churchill had been hidden in a Transvaal coal mine by a stout Mr. Dewsnap from Oldham. When Winston returned to the town in the Khaki Election of October, 1900, mill girls drew his carriage. Soon the EVENING CHRONICLE was congratulating him on " a plucky fight and a brilliant victory."

A few miles away, Liberals put out a poster—

Kruger's a Tory ; so is Balfour,
but Balfour won easily in East Manchester. Nothing could check the Conservative victory.

THE OFFICIAL NEWS.
Touching Messages.

The first official news of the death of the Queen, as we stated in our special late edition last night, came from the King in a message to the Lord Mayor of London, as follows:—

Osborne, Tuesday, 6-45 p.m.

The Prince of Wales to the Lord Mayor.
My beloved Mother the Queen has just passed away, surrounded by her children and grandchildren.

(Signed) ALBERT EDWARD.

The message from the doctors attendant the Queen was:—

Osborne, January 22, 1901, 6-45 p.m.

Her Majesty the Queen breathed her last at 6-30 p.m., surrounded by her children and grandchildren.

(Signed)
JAS. REID.
R. DOUGLAS POWELL.
THOMAS BARLOW.

In the following winter the old Queen died. The news was in the stop press of the evening papers of January 22nd, and the official bulletin was signed by a Lancashire man, Dr. Thomas Barlow, born at Bolton.

Buller came to the North-West in May, praising the Royal Lancs. and Lancs. Fusiliers as well as the Manchesters; the so-called Manchester Volunteers came home and the EVENING CHRONICLE published pictures of all their fallen. They numbered eleven.

Thereafter, the war again retreated towards the back of the paper, with W. G. Grace and MacLaren supplanting Kruger as the cartoonists' delight. The war had almost settled down to peace conditions.

On June 2nd, 1902, came news of the Boer surrender. There was little bitterness. The EVENING CHRONICLE expressed the prevailing mood in a cartoon showing John Bull offering his water flask to a fallen Boer. Beneath were the lines:

Old wrongs redressed, *the foe becomes our brother,*
Briton and Boer,
In battle taught to honour one another,
Shall strive no more.

London Road Station approach was lined with cheering crowds to welcome the Manchester Volunteers returning from the war

Scandals

"Few cities have in them so many thieves as Manchester. The pavement of Cottonopolis is increasingly trodden by rogues."

Detective Inspector Jerome Caminada, who delivered this verdict on the criminal condition of Manchester in the late nineties, was not given to understatement. But, just as Victorian London had its lurid underworld, so Manchester at the end of last century was not all its champions claimed.

In the year the EVENING CHRONICLE was founded a Home Office inquiry revealed grave scandals in the police and Watch Committee. The Chief Constable resigned and was succeeded by Robert Peacock, a one-time pie-shop keeper, who was able to report, in 1900, that "*only* 17 policemen had been reported drunk on duty in nine months."

PEACOCK, as Sydney and Beatrice Webb wrote, was "an ex-policeman, sturdy, independent, fairly alert, very oncoming." One of the first targets in his reform campaign was the Comedy Theatre, of which the lessee was J. Pitt Hardacre, famous as the man who bought the rights of " East Lynne " when others believed them to be worked out.

J. Pitt Hardacre

The police objected to renewal of the Comedy's licence and a city councillor, Edwyn Holt, said in effect that Hardacre's management was a scandal. A great action for slander followed. Hardacre engaged Marshall Hall, famous advocate and M.P. for Southport and, in the words of Hall's biographer, " the case threw a terrible light on the sordid life of a great city."

Marshall Hall did, however, succeed in damaging the police's evidence and, in a five hours' speech, nearly won the case. When the jury retired five were for Hardacre and seven for Holt. In the end they found a qualified verdict for the defendant.

The case was commented on by almost all national and provincial papers, and Hardacre, beaten but full of fight, carried on a running warfare with Peacock for years.

The struggle had some unforeseen effects. Peacock, who really did attack the city's vice racket, ended by becoming more powerful than any of the city's chief constables.

And Marshall Hall was unfairly denounced in Southport as " the man in the Comedy case," a display of mud-slinging which helped to bring about his defeat at the polls and retirement from politics.

"Arsenic in Beer"

THIS was the big scare of 1900 which resulted, for a time, in considerable compulsory teetotalism rather than temperance.

Much illness and many deaths occurred in Lancashire and Cheshire. A sudden, rapid increase in the number of hospital patients suffering from the kind of paralysis associated with excessive drinking first drew attention to the trouble.

Ultimately it was discovered that the trouble was due to the use of glucose and invert sugar made from impure sulphuric acid containing arsenic. The brewers recalled their supplies, stopped sales, held hundreds of barrels in quarantine and emptied thousands of gallons into the sewers.

A Royal Commission was appointed to investigate the matter, but by then beer drinkers had accepted the brewers' guarantee of the purity of their products and resumed normal imbibition.

The horseless carriages of 1901. Pioneers of a new age ready for the start of an early motoring trial

WHEN the EVENING CHRONICLE was founded, Lancashire folk still travelled by steam and horse. Within ten years a mechanical revolution was far advanced.

Blackpool was the first town in Britain to run electric trams in 1885, but progress was slow until about 1901 when Manchester scrapped its horse trams. Within six years the electric tram had spread throughout the urban North. It was possible to travel by it from Rochdale to Liverpool—fare 2s.; time, nine hours.

MOTOR 'BUS BOOM.

THE GREAT MANCHESTER SCHEME.

POWERFUL COMPANY FORMING.

MR. D. BOYLE AS MANAGING DIRECTOR

SUBURBAN DISTRICTS TO BE OPENED UP.

In spite of the reticence which has been maintained with regard to the inauguration

Electricity seemed to be the answer to most of man's transport problems. It enjoyed a false spring on the North's railways when the $18\frac{1}{2}$ miles of line between Liverpool and Southport were electrified in March, 1904.

"Electricity will take some time to displace steam on the great trunk lines," said the EVENING CHRONICLE, but it clearly expected that to happen. When there was a crash on the electrified line on July 28th, 1905, it again spoke of electricity as "the motive power now rapidly succeeding steam on the railways."

The real revolution, unsuspected at first, was on the roads. By 1904, motor-cars—at first jokingly called "mo-cars"—had really arrived.

In the same year Blackpool had a brilliant idea for making known its new promenade. This was, as the EVENING CHRONICLE said, "an ideal racing track," and on it the North's first big motor meeting was held. Over 250 competitors, "driving open-throttled cars, noisy as gatling-guns and with flames blazing from exhausts, daily risked their lives to set up fresh world speed records."

A minor revolution was also going on in newspapers. The half-tone process block came in, and the press-photographer began to oust the artist. The EVENING CHRONICLE's earliest half-tone blocks appeared in 1902, *on Saturdays only*, one of the first being of Sydney Barnes, the cricketer, wearing a moustache and straw hat.

Traffic Jam, 1911

THE MANCHESTER EVENING CHRONICLE. FRIDAY. JULY 28. 1

ELECTRIC RAILWAY CATASTROPHE

ON THE LIVERPOOL-SOUTHPORT SYSTEM

MORE THAN 20 PERSONS HURLED TO DEATH.

GRAPHIC NARRATIVES BY SURVIVORS:

PATHETIC INCIDENTS OF THE COLLISION

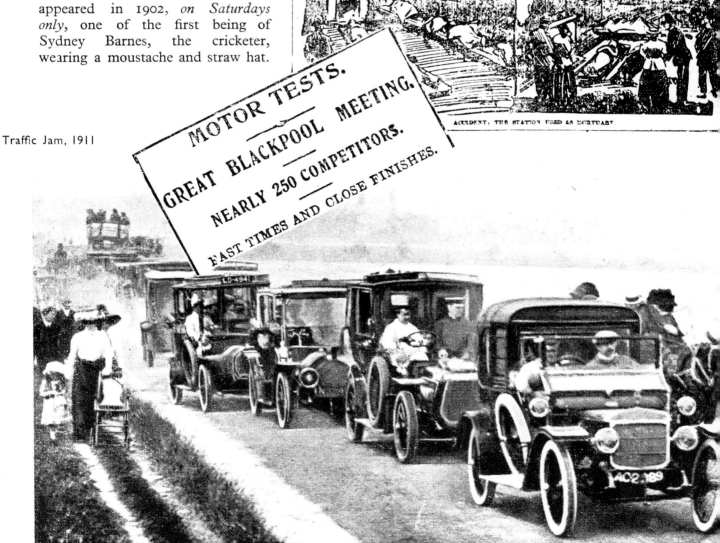

ACCIDENT. THE STATION USED AS MORTUARY.

MOTOR TESTS.

GREAT BLACKPOOL MEETING.

NEARLY 250 COMPETITORS.

FAST TIMES AND CLOSE FINISHES.

Edwardian

Skirts floppily flowing, waists of 20 inches, Gaiety Girls, bachelor girls, " The Merry Widow " . . . Men in choker collars or cloth caps . . . Motoring, smart high life, long week-ends, money to burn and a trip from Manchester to Blackpool for 3s.

Is this family album portrait of the Edwardian England correct? So far as it goes, yes. As Miss Rose Macaulay has said of the period: " There was more pleasure for those who could afford it; life had not been so gay for some time."

But except for the wealthy, led by a dignified, pleasure-loving king, the ascent to the Edwardian zenith was a gradual, less gaudy affair. In the early 1900's there was a good deal of trade depression in the North-West. Some towns, Widnes for instance, actually suffered a decline in population. Unemployment followed; workless rioted in Manchester in 1905, and the EVENING CHRONICLE came to their aid. It started a Penny Fund which rapidly raised some thousands of pounds—much to the envy of Sheffield's unemployed who repeated the old tag: " They manage these things better in Manchester."

In the second half of the decade things improved. Old Age Pensions came in and Churchill and Beveridge opened the first unemployment exchanges. There were still mill strikes and lock-outs—one lasted seven weeks in 1908—but on the whole Cotton was King again, and a prosperous monarch to boot. There were years of good trade and low prices. Manchester's rates hovered between 6s. and 7s. in the pound; Harris tweed suits cost 55s., Oldham mill workers had guinea trips to Paris and smoked cigars at seven for 1s.

Preoccupation with smartness, leisure and pleasure filtered down from the wealthy to the workers—but not without protest. Symptomatic was an indignant correspondence which raged in the EVENING CHRONICLE through June and July, 1907.

It began with an article by Nancy Yates who, after saying: " The mill girl does not always wear her clogs and shawl," went on to describe one in East Lancashire who spent £39 in a year on clothes, amusements and holidays.

This stung to the quick old-fashioned folk and poorly-paid workers. They treated it not as an example of improvidence but as a moral issue. It was felt that the good name of mill girls had been smirched.

" MERRY WIDOW " HAT DANGER.

Worse Than Sweep's Brush, Says Solicitor.

Trafford Park, now a huge industrial estate, was an expanse of fields and shady trees less than 50 years ago.

ʌʙᴏᴠᴇ : Market Place

Right : Bull's Head yard

"A mill girl's calling is as noble and pure as any," wrote one correspondent. "Some people think that if a girl goes out in her shawl and clogs she is not up to much," protested a second.

A third told Nancy Yates bluntly : "I should not like to be you if you was to come into our mill. You would feel somebody's clog before you had been in five minutes."

What particularly incensed these readers was the suggestion that a mill girl should spend 30s. on a fur and muff.

To crown the argument on what was seemly for a mill girl a St. Annes landlady declared : "The mill girl should go to her proper place —Blackpool. St. Annes was meant for her betters."

The mill girl probably preferred Blackpool

Later famous as a film actor, W. C. Fields appeared in Manchester as a juggler in the early days of the century

anyway. At home, and when she was not too tired, she contented herself with an occasional dance, a visit to the music hall or to the cinema which, from being a lodger in any sort of hall, was becoming a householder in its own right.

The stage was beginning to be regarded as less of a scandal and more as an opportunity. What, for instance, could be more romantic

The first headline of the
Evening Chronicle's "stage gossip"

THE theatre boomed and the EVENING CHRONICLE started a weekly two-column feature devoted entirely to it. This first appeared on March 16th, 1907, under the name of "Buccaneer," which lightly masked the identity of Mr. W. Buchanan Taylor.

Mr. W. Buchanan Taylor,
the first "Buccaneer"

than the rise of "Little Elsie"? In a few years she passed from singing in the London and North-Western Hotel, Salford, to queening it as Lily Elsie, loveliest of all "Merry Widows?"

When George Edwardes showed her to Franz Lehar, the composer demurred: "She look more like ze merry widow's daughter." She herself had, at first, a hearty Lancashire dislike of London, and was not very eager to take the part.

Within a year audiences would rise in their seats and shout in unison: "We all love Lily Elsie," and Royalty, home-grown and foreign, flocked to Daly's. One king saw the show twice a week.

It typified Edwardian notions about success, beauty, luxury and a good time.

Lily Elsie as
"The Merry Widow,"
1907

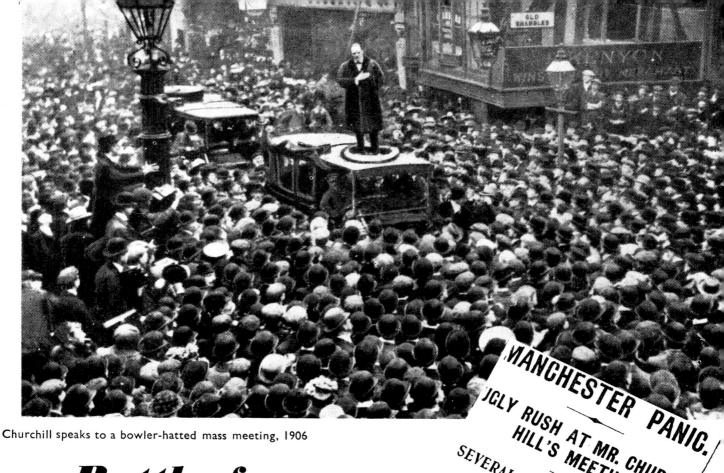

Churchill speaks to a bowler-hatted mass meeting, 1906

Battle for Free Trade

IN 1846 a Lancashire agitation and a Lancashire Prime Minister, Sir Robert Peel, made Britain a Free Trade country. Sixty years later Joseph Chamberlain challenged that decision and set out to reverse it. He called for Protection.

Nobody found this more embarrassing than did Arthur James Balfour, Prime Minister of the day. His sceptical mind doubted whether any single doctrine could ever be an economic cure-all—and for 20 years he had been M.P. for East Manchester in the heart of Free Trade's citadel.

In January, 1906, the Conservatives, divided among themselves, appealed to the country. Manchester's answer was brief and brusque. It was summed up by an EVENING CHRONICLE cartoon showing the electoral gramophone shouting "Free Trade, Free Trade!" Balfour lost his seat and the EVENING CHRONICLE'S comment on it was headed: "The Passing of Arthur."

MANCHESTER PANIC.

UGLY RUSH AT MR. CHURCH-
HILL'S MEETING.

SEVERAL PEOPLE INJURED

AND TAKEN TO INFIRMARY.

A serious accident marred the conclusion of Mr. Churchill's meeting this afternoon at the Coal Exchange.

Immediately Mr. Churchill had finished

HIS MA

Mr. Hilaire Belloc
(A Matt sketch)

This general election sent to Parliament many men who were to become famous in the next 40 years. Philip Snowden was returned at Blackburn and J. R. Clynes began his long reign in Miles Platting.

Newspaper comment on the candidates was candid, personal. The EVENING CHRONICLE described Clynes as "the little pale-faced warhorse of the labour movement," and labelled Hilaire Belloc, victorious in Salford, as "plain in appearance"—a verdict which a cartoon by Matt did nothing to upset.

To one rising politician, sundered from Conservatism by the Tariff issue, the campaign was a triumphal progress which did, indeed, include a torchlight procession up Cheetham Hill. Winston Churchill, still popularly known as "The Boy," had an easy victory in North-West Manchester. The impression he made can be gauged from the EVENING CHRONICLE's gallery of pictures of victorious candidates. Beneath each a brief biography appeared. There was one exception. Churchill's portrait carried only a caption : SPEAKS FOR HIMSELF.

Mr. J. R. Clynes, once a mill-worker at Oldham, as he looked at the beginning of a political career in which he reached the top of the tree

"Rimington"

"FRANCIS DUCKWORTH of Colne," is the description always given to the composer of "Rimington." He lived in Colne, but he was born in the little Ribblesdale village whose name he gave to the most popular hymn tune composed in the 20th century.

During his boyhood at Rimington he listened to a debate in his father's shop about the merits of hymn writers. Duckworth's uncle preferred Isaac Watts above all others and, carried away by enthusiasm, he raised his hand in a mighty flourish and, in a deep, eloquent voice recited the line "Jesus shall reign where'er the sun." "Ah," he said, "Watts said more in one line than your modern hymn writers can say in a whole hymn."

This, and the look of admiration on his uncle's face, overwhelmed the boy with a longing to compose a tune to Watts' great words. Years later, in Colne, he carried out his design. "Rimington" was published in 1904. It won immediate and lasting success. Over 3,000,000 copies of it are in circulation to-day. It is included in ten English and eight foreign hymnals.

"Rimington" has cheered a handful of lonely people on Pitcairn Island, and served as a hymn of victory. After the capture of Jerusalem in 1917, a party of Lancashire Fusiliers marched to Mount Calvary and, halting on the summit, sang "Rimington."

Francis Duckworth at the harmonium

VAUDEVILLE and "LEGIT."

1897 — 1914

IRVING

BERNHARDT

PATRICK CAMPBELL

ALEXANDER

MARK SHERIDAN

MARIE LLOYD

VESTA TILLEY

GEORGE GRAVES

Above: WILKIE BARD

Left: GEORGE FORMBY (Senr.)

ANNIE HORNIMAN, foundress of the Gaiety Theatre

Birth of a Tradition

In 1907 a company of Irish players from the Abbey Theatre, Dublin, came to Manchester, giving plays by J. M. Synge and W. B. Yeats at the Midland Theatre. Their backer and mentor was an ardent-eyed woman in early middle age, Miss Annie Horniman who, in her own words, " had observed her elders in her early youth and by their disapproval became interested in the theatre."

That visit to Manchester was decisive for her and for the history of the English theatre. It struck her that there was about the Lancashire folk " something downright and solid that seemed to promise success."

She decided to found England's first repertory theatre among them.

She did so at the Gaiety Theatre in April, 1908, staying there 13 years, producing 200 plays, over 100 of them original.

In red silk or green brocade, with a great plaque of opals gleaming on her breast, Annie Horniman was a striking figure. Her theatre was less sumptuous. She banished gilt from the decorations and brass from the orchestra, and boasted about it, a little artily, a little snobbishly. In a period of material prosperity there was charm in the Horniman " austerity."

What really made the Gaiety, however, was not its arty appeal to local intellectuals but the excellence of its early actors and actresses and the adventurousness of its choice of plays. Miss Horniman set herself to encourage local writers. First in point of time was H. M. Richardson, leader writer of the EVENING CHRONICLE. The Gaiety produced half a dozen of his plays before he turned his back on the stage to become General Secretary of the National Union of Journalists, founded in Lancashire about the same time as the Horniman " Rep."

Next came a young, unknown man, still in his twenties—Stanley Houghton. He looked like a nascent genius, and for a short time England really believed he was one when, in 1912, he wrote " Hindle Wakes," most famous of Lancashire plays. It won immediate, immense success—and 18 months later its lionized author lay dead in his home in Athol Street, Alexandra Park.

The triumph of " Hindle Wakes " was high noon in the fortunes of the Gaiety players. But there had been many notable successes before that. There was a first-rate comedy, " Hobson's Choice," by Harold Brighouse ; and Allan Monkhouse, technically the most accomplished of the so-called " Lancashire school," showed himself a real artist in " Mary Broome."

Then there were many famous plays by continental dramatists and an abundance of Galsworthy and Shaw, notwithstanding the fact that Miss Horniman and G.B.S. used to " spar fearfully." She was more than a match for him. She had a beautiful knack of turning the tables on an opponent; for instance, when " Hindle Wakes " was banned at Oxford on moral grounds, she did not criticize the Vice-Chancellor. She slyly said: " I shall pray for him."

But between the Gaiety's artistic peaks there were flat plains, tedious to all but the elect. "Time after time," complained Richard Prentis, " the curtain would go up on a Welsh dresser and a kitchen table with Sybil weeping in frustration. Sometimes the dresser would be to the left, sometimes to the right. But the table and Sybil were constant."

Sybil's surname was Thorndike, one of the great company which shone at the Gaiety in its opening years. Others were Maire O'Neill, Sarah Allgood, Miss Darragh, Iden Payne, Lewis Casson, Basil Dean and Herbert Lomas.

For five years the Gaiety was the most dynamic force in the English theatre. Then it faltered. Some blamed the Manchester public; some Miss Horniman's choice of plays and her determination to edify her audiences.

The " civilized theatre," as she was fond —too fond— of calling it, survived until 1921, when the foundress departed. Her last words were : " If the Gaiety should ever become a boudoir for the movies . . ." It promptly did become that. But the repertory movement spread outwards from Manchester and lived on, the abiding legacy of the Horniman experiment.

The climax of " Hindle Wakes." Fanny, the millgirl, refuses to marry the millowner's son. A photograph of the first production by the Horniman Company at the Playhouse, London, 1912

Above: H. C. Lomax, "Bayard" of the *Sunday Chronicle*, who became part owner of the touring rights of " Hindle Wakes '

EDYTHE GOODALL   ADA KING   LEONARD MUDIE   H. LOMAS   DAISY ENGLAND   J. N. BRYANT

Matt

MATT SANDFORD, probably the best caricaturist who ever worked in Manchester, came from Belfast to join the EVENING CHRONICLE in the early 1900's.

To abundant native wit he added exceptional powers of observation and

Lord Morley, of Blackburn (1838-1923), famous statesman and litterateur. Wrote the standard life of his friend, Gladstone. Known as "Honest John," he sat in many Liberal Cabinets until August, 1914, when, as a strong pacifist, he resigned

Hans Richter (1843-1916), Wagner's right-hand man and famous conductor. Settled in Manchester following the foundation of the Hallé Concerts Society by Gustav Behrens, 1898. Excelled in the German classics. Resigned amid controversy, 1911

memory. He was able to seize the salient features of whole groups of people and recall instantly details of any contest in the country at the preceding general election.

This, and his flair for dashing off lightning sketches, made him a popular turn at entertainments. His admirers held he might rival Datas on the halls, and some of them wanted to float him as a limited company. But the idea failed to appeal to Matt. He was an artist first and foremost.

Charles Rowley (1839-1933), of Ancoats. Spent 70 years working for the welfare of "the highest death-rate part of the highest death-rate city." Friend of many great Victorians from Rossetti to Shaw. A human, humorous, unselfish man

Bishop Welldon (1854-1937), Dean of Manchester 1906-1918. A big man in every sense of the word. Genial, impulsive and a man of multifarious interests, he was a powerful preacher and a first-rate public speaker. Immensely popular with working men

"The Fat Boy"

The Royal Exchange is the " Fat Boy " of Manchester buildings. During the past century it has rarely been deemed big enough for its purpose for more than a score of years at a time.

Six times since it was first opened in 1729 it has been rebuilt or extended. The third Exchange (bottom, right) was built 1867-1874 and was thought to have solved the accommodation problem for all time. But as the Poy cartoon (right) shows it was again judged too small in the 1900's.

Between 1914 and 1921 it was drastically reconstructed, almost the only remaining external part of the old Exchange being the tower. The building, covering 1.7 acres, was opened by King George V on Oct. 8th, 1921.

The blitz of 1940 again cramped the men who go on 'Change and a start is to be made this year on yet another reconstruction — the seventh.

WANTED---A 'CHANGE.

CHORUS OF MEMBERS : "Good gracious! He's bursting out of 'em. We must give him another 'change'!"

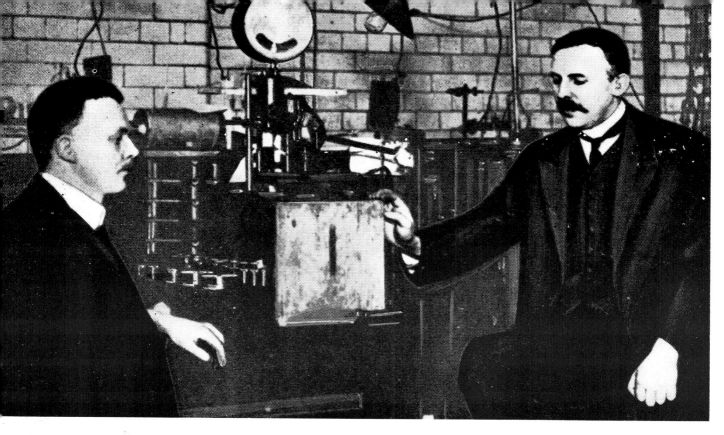

Rutherford (right) and Geiger in the Physics Laboratory of Manchester University

Rutherford

" He is the one man living who promises to confer some inestimable boon on mankind as a result of my own discovery of radium."

THE speaker was Madame Curie, the subject, Ernest Rutherford, Langworthy Professor of Physics at Manchester University. This great scientist came to Manchester in 1907 and in the next 12 years laid bare the foundations of that knowledge which, when the first atom bombs fell on Japan, put an abrupt end to the Second World War.

At its most pregnant moments science is apt to be outwardly as unspectacular, as invisible almost as the atom itself. What Manchester saw of Rutherford was a big, bluff, shaggy man who looked like a farmer. A superficially simple man who, when things went well with his work, strode along whistling " Onward, Christian Soldiers " or, when things went not so well, " Fight the Good Fight."

Beneath this exterior worked one of the most potent brains Lancashire has ever known. Rutherford had brilliant helpers in Manchester—Geiger, H. G. J. Moseley (killed in the Dardanelles landings), and Neils Bohr, who helped the Allies to evolve the atom bomb. But—to use the language of physics—they were the electrons of Manchester's scientific " atom." Its nucleus— the central positively charged particle—was Rutherford, and his years at Manchester have been described by his biographer as the greatest period of his life.

During them he made two great discoveries. The first, revealed to the Manchester Literary and Philosophical Society in 1911, was the constitution of the atom. The second was the means of producing artificial disintegration of the atom. In 1917, after he had disrupted a nitrogen nucleus, he said : " We might expect to break down the nuclear structure of many of the lighter atoms."

His modest " might " has become an ominous certainty. We still await the inestimable boon predicted by Madame Curie. But it will come.

Poy

THE "ELECTOR" IN POLL—AR REGIONS.

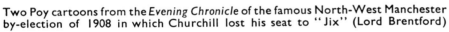

Reconnoitring the "North-West" Passage.

Two Poy cartoons from the *Evening Chronicle* of the famous North-West Manchester by-election of 1908 in which Churchill lost his seat to "Jix" (Lord Brentford)

Poy, by Matt

His real name is Percy H. Fearon. It served him as a youngster in Shanghai where he was born. Later, while he was living in the U.S.A., his friends translated it into Americanese—"Poysy." Finally Britain made it Poy. Nothing could be more appropriate. Poy rhymes with Joy—and Poy provided Joy for millions.

His cartoons, which first graced the EVENING CHRONICLE in the 1900's were all-Poy. He invented the ideas, the comic situations, the characters, including The Little Man in the Bowler Hat—a creation that sometimes was credited elsewhere.

HOME AGAIN.

RETURNED WANDERER (with an anxious eye on the kennel): "I w-wonder if absence has made the heart grow fonder!"

(Mr. Winston Churchill, M.P., is expected to arrive in England to-day.)

The first British aeroplane. Sir A. V. Roe's biplane at Brooklands in 1908

Below : The designer seated in his machine in the year of his first 60-yards flight

Henry Farman's kite-like biplane was the wonder of England's first flying meeting at Blackpool, 1909. Below he is seen winning the long distance flight (47 miles)

"Dangerous...

Sᴇᴀsɪᴅᴇ folk usually prefer a holiday inland. But when they take a jaunt in mid-August you can be certain that there's business mixed with the pleasure.

At that date in 1909, a party from Blackpool, headed by Alderman John Bickerstaffe, were on the plain of Bethany, near Rheims. French aviators, then the best in the world, were holding their first big flying meeting.

Would they, asked the men from Lancashire, come to England? Yes, they would. The visitors hurried home and organized England's first flying meeting, held at Blackpool, October 18th—23rd, 1909.

In those days aeroplanes were not much more than outsize kites with an engine and a basket chair for the pilot. But the Frenchmen made light of danger, flew in gales, won big prizes and—pretty often—broke their necks.

Headed by Farman, Paulhan, Latham, Le Blanc and Rougier they flocked to Blackpool, where Farman astonished the Northerners by flying 47 miles, a performance described by the Eᴠᴇɴɪɴɢ Cʜʀᴏɴɪᴄʟᴇ as "A Great Triumph."

Tʜᴀᴛ sounds comic to-day. But it was a beginning—and more than English airmen were capable of for the time being. How native flying was faring can be judged from the misadventures of a young Mancunian, Mr. A. V. Roe.

. . . foredoomed to Failure"

From 1902 he had been making model flying machines—and was heavily rebuked by the *Times* for experiments which it described as "Not only dangerous to human life but foredoomed to failure." He answered the *Times* on June 8th, 1908, by producing the first English plane ever to fly. It went 60 yards at an altitude of 2 ft.

He named this plane Bull Dog No. 1 and took it to Blackpool together with an improved model, Bull Dog No. 2, fitted with a four-cylinder J.A.P. engine. How he fared that week can be judged from the EVENING CHRONICLE'S report:

Beyond leaving the ground for some 15 yards his efforts have been barren of results.

But he persevered until the meeting was abandoned owing to bad weather. "At that point," said the EVENING CHRONICLE reporter, "Mr. Roe's face was a study in mortification."

He had at last got Bull Dog No. 2 ready for flying.

BLACKPOOL had a second aviation meeting the following year, when the hero was Claude Grahame-White. He not only landed on Blackpool sands on a Bank Holiday week-end afternoon—a feat never repeated—but said : "I'll go to Southport." And he did.

Before this happened the most famous of all pioneer British flying races had been held. It ended at 5-30 a.m., April 28th, 1910, when Paulhan landed in a clover field at Burnage. He won the £10,000 prize offered by Lord Northcliffe to the first man to fly from London to Manchester, and he did the 186 miles in 5 hours 8 minutes—with a break at Lichfield during which he slept seven hours.

At Burnage, Madame Paulhan flung her arms round the victor, and Paulhan told the EVENING CHRONICLE : "My machine flew splendidly, but it was so cold, so very cold. I would not do it again for £20,000."

Mancunians, elated and excited, flocked to Burnage where the only man not in good spirits was Farmer Matthew Bracegirdle. He registered an emphatic protest.

FLYING MAN AND THE FARMER.

Burnage Man and Damage to His Crops.

EMPHATIC PROTEST.

"Landing in His Field Without Permission."

Mr. Matthew Bracegirdle, the farmer of Fogg-lane, Burnage, on whose field M. Paulhan.

Paulhan in his prime

Below : The victor with his wife and Farman after the first London to Manchester flight, April, 1910

The End of an Era

ON May 7th, 1910, King Edward VII died and, in the famous phrase, " England went black in a night."

It was our last display of total national mourning, and it may be taken as a dividing line between periods, for the temper of the new decade was darker than that of the 1900's.

Five days after the King's funeral the EVENING CHRONICLE reported the Bishop of London's views on divorce. He did not merely attack it; he said that " the facilities enjoyed by the rich must never be extended to the poor."

This kind of angry dogmatism, culminating in Carson's " Ulster has a moral right to use force," was growing. It blazed out in the things Lloyd George said about the rich—and in the things doctors said about Lloyd George and his " panel." It even showed itself in controversy about the Hallé Concerts programmes.

LED by Jack Kahane, who first published his views in the *Daily Dispatch*, a group of champions of modern music attacked the aged, famous Richter, the Hallé conductor, for his supposed musical conservatism.

KING EDWARD'S LAST HOURS

Unconscious of the Presence o
The Royal Family.

PATHETIC GRIEF OF THE QUEE

Many Messages Being Received
Foreign Rulers.

TO-DAY'S SCENES AT THE PALACE

It is a blood red track, the track of the exception of the
Halley's comet. The comet comes regu- Queen Maud, on re
at long intervals; but just as announcing the crit
its appearance been father, replied at o
that has thrown for London and wo
Sunday.

By January, 1911, they had passed beyond verbal controversy. They held up a concert by protracted and ironic applause. Richter, massive and impassive, ignored the demonstrators—but he resigned the following month. Only a straw in the wind, yet it showed the mood of the time.

IT was present again in the two general elections of 1910. When Churchill described Bonar Law as " raw material," it provoked from the Conservative leader not repartee but an indignant, if controlled, justification of his career. From his little note-book Bonar Law quoted facts and figures impressively, but he failed to top the poll in North-West Manchester.

A few days later came the first of a series of big disasters which dogged these years.

Between the 1880's and 1914 thousands of Northerner
were spurred on to read the classics through buyin
" Lewis's Penny Readings." Here is the cover of th
1912 issue. It contained 128 pages and 100 selections fror
authors from Shakespeare to Kipling

"Lancashire is to spend a sorrowful Christmas," said the EVENING CHRONICLE on December 21st. At Little Hulton, near Bolton, over 340 miners lost their lives in the county's greatest mining disaster. In ten days, readers of the paper subscribed £5,500 for the dead men's wives and children.

Labour disputes grew fiercer. On March 1st, 1912, Britain's miners downed tools and the EVENING CHRONICLE headlines read:

NATIONAL COAL STRIKE
COTTON MILLS COMPELLED
TO CLOSE ALREADY.

Evidently in those days of cheap, abundant coal, some mills never troubled to carry stocks.

IT must not, however, be thought that in general this was a gloomy period. Prices were low, holidays merry, roller skating was the craze, and the *Daily Sketch* promoted the North's first big beauty competition. In the music halls George Formby, sen. was at his zenith; Florrie Forde was singing "Dear Old Pal" and "Put on your ta-ta." Other hits were "Ship Ahoy," "Fall in and Follow me," "Joshua," "Kelly from the Isle of Man," and "Beautiful Garden of Roses."

Movement in men's fashions continued to be glacial, but women's grew freakish, ephemeral. Hair was dressed over pads; obvious make-up was still considered "fast"; stockings were always black, usually cashmere, rarely silk. Hats were, at first, enormous. Their wearers had to sidle like crabs to get on trams. "Is my hat on straight?" became a catch phrase.

Considering what happened to women's fashions ten years later, an EVENING CHRONICLE article of July 17th, 1913, makes quaint reading.

The Wizard in the Welsh hills. Mr. and Mrs. Lloyd George were camping on Moel Hebog with "Little Megan" when an *Evening Chronicle* photographer took this picture in 1913

MAKE FREAK COSTUMES USEFUL?

THE FASHIONS OF WOMEN OF TO-

An Artist on Craze For Less Clothing.

DRESS AND UNDRESS.

Ladies Best Judges of Their Own Styles.

Has the undress craze in modern fashions gone too far? Are we to see a re

any man or woman ashamed at seeing the beauty of the human figure accentuated by dress.

MANCHESTER GIRLS.

"In the old days they had some pride in the human frame and physique. On the Continent they found it out long ago. English people are only just waking up to it, and whether it is the directoire, the slash, or any other style, let us have it used, of course in conjunction with

ng young girls in ceeded. "has

"Has the undress craze in modern fashions gone too far?" it asked. "Women nowadays wear almost nothing under their gowns, even in daytime. Petticoats went some time back. . . ."

AGAINST this social background, George V began his reign. In Manchester his Coronation Day opened tepidly. The only cheer was for a parade of Crimean and

Mutiny veterans. Even at the firing of a Royal Salute in Platt Fields somebody blundered and the R.F.A., after trying for an hour to secure firing space, rode back sulkily to H.Q. The police then cleared a space and the gunners were induced to return. By night, the Coronation spirit had risen; omnibus men who had been plying vainly quickly filled up at 3d. a time for the bonfires on Alms Hill.

In vivid contrast was the rousing welcome given the King and Queen two years later when they made a Royal Progress, visiting almost every Lancashire town south of Blackpool and Colne. Everywhere they were fêted and cheered, especially in the mills.

At one of them, near Blackburn, they caught a last glimpse of a vanishing Lancashire. It was of 80-years'-old Richard Radcliffe weaving on a 100-years'-old hand-loom, while his wife, Ellen, span cops by his side.

King George V and Queen Mary on the steps of Manchester Town Hall in July, 1913, when the Lord Mayor, Sir Samuel Royse, received the accolade in public

Sir Harry Lauder famous Scots comedian, a popular visitor, photographed in Manchester, in September, 1913

ROYAL PROGRESS

King George V and Queen Mary driving through Liverpool during a lengthy visit to Lancashire
in 1913. Facing them in the carriage are Lord Derby (left), and the present King, then known as
Prince Albert

Titanic

"It is with the deepest and most profound regret that we have to record the fact that news of the rescue of the passengers of the White Star leviathan *Titanic* . . . has proved incorrect."

That was how, through the columns of the EVENING CHRONICLE for April 16th, 1912, Lancashire learnt of the greatest disaster in sea history. With the possible exception of the *Queen Mary*, no liner has ever sailed from Britain on her maiden voyage amid so much national pride as the *Titanic*. This floating luxury palace was something new in ships. She was unsinkable. The experts said so.

So when, on April 15th, it was reported that the great liner had struck an iceberg off Cape Race, the public was more curious than alarmed. From New York the owners of the ship reported that " all passengers have been rescued." The EVENING CHRONICLE interviewed experts. They were unanimous. "No danger." "Absolutely unsinkable."

The terrible truth was that, amidst scenes of heartrending panic, the *Titanic* had gone down with the loss of 1,500 lives.

The English-speaking world was appalled at this confounding of human pride ; it was angered by disclosure that the ship was under-equipped with boats, and it was dismayed by stories of survivors who, having got into the boats, offered the sailors money not to return to rescue others.

But there was one story of heroism aboard the *Titanic* that stirred all Britain. It was the account of the ship's band and their Lancashire bandmaster, Wallace Hartley, of Colne. All refused to quit their posts. To keep up the spirits of the passengers they played cheerful music — waltzes, popular songs.

Then, when the doom of the ship was certain, Hartley rallied his men and called upon them to play

Nearer my God to Thee,
Nearer to Thee . . .

He was still playing when the vast ship turned on end and plunged beneath the waves.

Suffragettes

"SUFFRAGETTES" . . . The word to-day is faded, remote and slightly ridiculous—like the harem skirt or the hobble skirt. But in 1913 it was sensational, sinister, boring.

The story of the battle for women's suffrage runs like a serial story through the pages of the EVENING CHRONICLE for a decade before the First World War.

It began with a little meeting of unknown women in Manchester, in 1903. They banded themselves together in the Women's Social and Political Union under the leadership of a delicately built, prettily dressed widow, Mrs. Emmeline Pankhurst.

Mrs. Pankhurst was registrar of Chorlton-on-Medlock, a £250-a-year post to which she had been helped by powerful friends when her barrister husband died prematurely in 1898, leaving her poorly-off.

When the Women's Social and Political Union began to criticize the Government of the day the Registrar-General told its leader it was "undesirable" for her to indulge in politics. She had to resign her registrarship.

Not many disciplinary acts have proved more expensive for Authority. Mrs. Pankhurst began to organize the suffrage movement on a militant model. That was in 1908, and in the next six years she was in and out of gaol a dozen times, sometimes with one or more of her daughters, sometimes without. The girls' names were Christabel and Sylvia.

AT first the "Shrieking Sisterhood" were looked upon as a joke. That was possible so long as they went no further than padlocking themselves to railings, heckling at Mr. Churchill's meetings or kicking an amiable Cabinet Minister, Augustine Birrell, on the shins.

But the little widow from Lancashire was grimly earnest. "We need to fight men like men—that is to say with violence," she cried.

Under the spell of her oratory women, married and single—but mostly single—were eager not only to give money and jewels, but to break the law whenever she gave the order, ploughing up golf courses, cutting telegraph wires,.burning houses, and even committing suicide by throwing themselves under the hooves of racehorses.

Truly might a Manchester acquaintance of Mrs. Pankhurst tell the EVENING CHRONICLE: "She is a pleasant person to meet, but a very dangerous woman to cross."

Main centre of the disturbances was London where raids could be made on Parliament, bricks heaved at Mr. Asquith, and £5,000 worth of windows smashed in the West End in a few hours.

But Manchester, where the Pankhursts first fell foul of the police, had its own suffragette "terror"—window smashing, attacks on trains and signal boxes, the pouring of black liquid into postal pillar boxes and so on.

The campaign had its recurrent bouts of comedy, as when Dame Ethel Smyth, composer of the militants' "March of the Women," was gaoled. Sir Thomas Beecham visited her and, looking through a window, saw in the prison quadrangle some stalwart young women marching round and round singing, "while Dame Ethel conducted this glorious band of Amazons with a toothbrush."

BUT in between the laughs Authority was kept on the jump. When the Royal Progress through Lancashire began in 1913 the EVENING CHRONICLE's preliminary story was headed:

GUARDING THE KING IN MANCHESTER
Militants to be Watched

At the very height of the tour the police found in the house of a Manchester suffragette a tin of gunpowder, "a shell that could serve as a bomb," a revolver, a pistol, and black silk masks.

Women won the vote late in the First World War. By that time the suffragette movement was sick, probably dying. The war had given its zealots other things to do—and more than their fill of violence.

POLICE RAID.

Suffragists in Court.

CONSPIRACY CHARGE.

Alleged Leaders of the Recent Outrages.

THE WOMEN TALKED and the men listened and—generally—smiled at the cry: "VOTES FOR WOMEN," shouted insistently from 1908 to 1914. When Miss Sylvia Pankhurst (*above*) harangued a mass meeting in Stevenson Square, Manchester's "Hyde Park," her audience was mainly male. She wore a wide halo hat and, more than once her mother and sister, Christabel, wore broad arrows. They went to prison for their beliefs—and 20 years later Prime Minister Stanley Baldwin unveiled a statue to Mrs. Pankhurst.

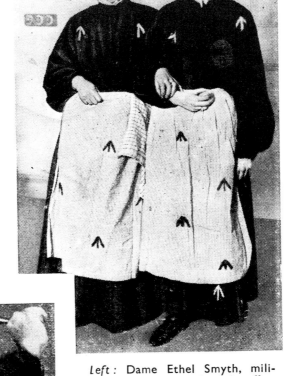

Left: Dame Ethel Smyth, militant musician, conducted suffragettes with a toothbrush. *Right:* Mrs. Pankhurst hugged off to prison, 1914

Murder at the Seaside

On the evening of Friday, December 12th, 1913, while the Crossley family of Regent Road, Blackpool, were at supper they saw a great stain of water on the ceiling. Upstairs, Mrs. Alice Smith, bride of their new lodger, was having a bath. They hesitated to grumble at Mrs. Smith, "a stout, merry nurse," so soon after her arrival in their home—and while they paused a human life was destroyed.

A few minutes later the bridegroom called out "Alice!" and then: "My wife will not speak to me." She was dead—and on the Monday a coroner's jury found that "The deceased suffered from heart disease and the cause of death was accidental."

In this disarming way passed by one of the stealthiest murders of all time. Only one person was suspicious. Mrs. Crossley was struck by the lack of grief shown by bridegroom Smith, and still more by the fact that he ordered his wife a pauper's funeral. She turned Smith out and wrote on a card upon which he had left his address: "Wife died in bath; we shall see him again."

She did see him again—in the summer of 1915, when George Joseph Smith stood trial for the murder of three of his wives, all of whom died in their baths. No one knows how Smith killed them. He was the "perfect murderer"—undone by repetition of his perfect formula.

"Tipperary"

JACK JUDGE

"It's a long way to . . ."

Jack Judge, a singer at the Grand Theatre, Stalybridge, in 1912, never caught the name of the place. But, as he walked home, between midnight and one a.m. on January 31st those words, spoken by one night roamer to another, gave him an idea that went round the world.

Jack had been spending the evening in a club with Frank Newbury, manager of a troupe of performing seals. It must have been a gay night for Jack bet five shillings that he would compose and sing a new song within 24 hours.

He hadn't a notion what it would be about so he pounced upon the words "It's a long way . . ." What happened then he explained years later to the editor of the *Stalybridge Year Book*.

"I added the word 'Tipperary,' did a little thinking until bedtime, and after a fish breakfast in the morning I completed the song in less time than it has taken me to tell you this story."

Below : George J. Smith with Miss Munday, daughter of a Wiltshire bank manager, who died in her bath at Herne Bay in July, 1912

1914

"The holiday outlook is very bright . . ." So ran an EVENING CHRONICLE caption to a bathing picture from New Brighton on July 31st, 1914.

Three days later Europe was at war. It was Bank Holiday Monday and the papers carried maps showing where France had been invaded. At Old Trafford a battle of a different kind was in progress. Red Rose and White were at grips when, suddenly, A. H. Hornby, the Lancashire captain, left the field. He had been called away by the War Office. Reggie Spooner and Sir Archibald White, the Yorkshire skipper, were also summoned, though by the time they went Yorkshire had won by ten wickets. The two captains never appeared on the ground again.

Two days later the embodiment of the East Lancs. Territorial Division was in full swing. The Lancashire Fusiliers were mobilizing at Bury, and by the end of the week Manchester and Salford became virtually garrison towns.

Camping grounds were opened at Rochdale, Bolton and Bury, and after 16 days of waiting 19,000 men and 7,000 horses were given an early morning send off as they marched away to begin their real training for foreign service.

The famous poster "Your King and Country Need You" appeared on the walls, and Lancashire responded nobly. By the end of the month came the Derby Scheme and the enlistment of thousands of city warehousemen and clerks into what became known as the " Pals " Battalions.

New and bigger buildings were requisitioned to cope with them, but thousands were turned away daily. Finally a crowd of 400 stormed the Manchester Town Hall to demand a quicker passing of recruits than one in 25 minutes.

Other things than recruiting were going on in those sunny, anxious days when the seemingly victorious Germans rolled towards Paris. Lord Derby opened Knowsley as a military hospital ; the Red Cross flag floated over Manchester Royal Infirmary, and Whitworth Street Municipal School also became a hospital.

There, early in September, arrived the first wounded—men of the 2nd Manchesters and the East Lancs. Regiment, and also some wounded German prisoners. Many of the British Tommies arrived with their belongings tied up in handkerchiefs. Their kit-bags had been left behind.

It was Lancashire's first close-up of war and war's meaning since the remnant of Bonnie Prince Charlie's army fled towards Carlisle in 1745.

While our men were pouring towards Mons, refugees from Belgium were fleeing in thousands to Britain. They were accorded almost royal honours. Crowds lined their routes, Lord Mayors and mayors competed to receive and refresh them. The earliest wave came from the villages around burnt Louvain, Aerschot and Malines, and for many months Lancashire continued to give sanctuary to these fugitives from the Hun.

The man who found the men and the man who used them. Lord Derby and Lord Kitchener at Manchester Town Hall

Under the Derby Scheme the prospect of going to war in company of your own choosing was made possible— every regiment had its Pals Battalions. Here Lord Kitchener is watching a march past from the steps of Manchester Town Hall

Momentarily the Kaiser's hordes were typified—however incongruously—for South Lancashire folk by Capt. Theodore Schlagintweit, noted socialite, hospitable *bon vivant* and German Consul in Manchester. He was first detained, then prosecuted for a breach of the Aliens Act, and finally arrested as a prisoner of war. While awaiting a military escort he was held at the Town Hall, a pathetic figure, at times in tears.

If Schlagintweit failed—except in popular fancy—to correspond with current portraits of Prussian militarism, a wounded Oldham postman certainly lived up the North's idea of an English hero.

The war "caught on" with the girls, too, and many unofficial bodies such as the Girl Signallers, seen here, sprang up before the W.A.A.C. was formed

Two days before Christmas he was told by the matron of a Macclesfield hospital that he had won the V.C.—the second of the war—for bravery at Festubert. He was John Hogan, a sergeant in the 2nd Manchesters. Like many a brave man before him, he later sold matches in Manchester's Market Street. He died in 1943 and was buried with regimental honours.

The Kaiser's Christmas card to England was a shell dropped in a Dover garden, while the wounded in hospitals made as merry as they could and received gifts of tobacco from the King and Queen and comforts from the Relief Organizations, which then abounded and were a prominent feature of Lancashire life at that time.

Continuing his 1915 tour, Kitchener went on to Liverpool

Wartime headlines

THE EVENING CHRONICLE, SATURDAY, MAY 8, 1915.

LOSS OF 1,457 LIVES IN THE LUSITANIA.
GERMANS GLOAT OVER THE MURDER OF WOMEN AND CHILDREN.

PLIGHT OF SURVIVORS

Three Hours in the Sea Before Rescuing Ships Arrive.

THRILLING NARRATIVES.

Captain Saved After Staying on the Bridge to the End

LINER TWICE TORPEDOED 15 FROM COAST.

703 SAVED.
Nearly 1500 Lives Lost.
OFFICIAL MESSAGES.

THE CAPTAIN RESCUED.
...shed from the Bridge.
...G STORIES.

SURVIVORS' NAMES.
Official List of the Saved.
RETURN INCOMPLETE.
Little Hope of Any Further Survivors.

GERMANS GLOAT.
"Satisfaction" of Officials.
"WARNING" TO U.S.A.

WORLD-WIDE HORROR.
"Germany Should Be Suppressed."

PREMEDITATED MURDERS.
Lord Derby
German Crime.
DUTY OF BRITONS
Appeal for Men to
Race of Assassins

TRAGIC SCENES AT QUEENSTOWN.

Pitiable Condition of the Rescued: Large Number of Bodies Landed.

LLOYD GEORGE GETS TO WORK.
Sends for Labour Party.
SEATS OFFERED.
Labour Demands Bigger Share.
ASQUITH'S MOVE.
Important Liberal Meeting To-morrow.

GERMAN DREAD OF LLOYD GEORGE.
His England Must Be Conquered.

FOOD POLICE NEXT
A New Terror of War Time.
CAFE MANAGER'S VIEWS.
Gluttons May be Hauled From the Table.

Our War Chief.

An Epic of Gallantry

WITHIN a month of the outbreak of World War No. 1, Manchester alone had provided 20,000 recruits. Other Lancashire towns responded with equal enthusiasm and eventually the county raised four Army Divisions, the 42nd, 55th, 57th and 66th.

Outstanding are the records of the 42nd in Egypt, Gallipoli and France and the magnificent defence of Givenchy by the 55th which drew a special order of the day from Sir Douglas Haig.

But the whole war record of the Lancashire regiments is an epic of gallantry. The Lancashire Fusiliers won 25 V.C.s, more than any regiment in the British Army. The Manchesters, who had 42 battalions in the war, won 11 V.Cs., and 72 battle honours, of which 10 are inscribed on the King's Colour. The Loyal Regiment (North Lancs.) were awarded 68 battle honours.

THE 1st Battalion King's Own Royal Regiment (Lancaster) was in France in August, 1914, facing the Prussian Guards and the 2nd Battalion, brought from India, served first in France, where Hancourt and Ypres were the scenes of much bitter and gallant fighting, and later in Macedonia.

The 4th Battalion of the East Lancs. Regiment drawn mainly from Blackburn, Darwen and Clitheroe, and the 5th Battalion from Burnley, Accrington, Haslingden and Bacup, went with the East Lancashire Brigade to the Near East.

They were at Cape Helles, Gallipoli, in 1915, and two years later were on the Somme, in the third battle of Ypres, and at Nieuport, La Bassee and Gommecourt.

The Accrington Pals went first to the Suez Canal and afterwards to France, attacking Ploegsteert Wood where the 1st Battalion made history in the early days of the war. The 6th Battalion was at Anzac Cove, the 7th and 8th in France, and the 9th at Salonika and the Dardanelles.

Conquest by Limelight

CHRISTMAS 1916, the middle of the war, and the curtain falling at the Prince's Theatre, Manchester, while an ecstatically enthusiastic audience cheered themselves hoarse.

It was the first night of "The Maid of the Mountains," billed as "the latest George Edwardes musical production." But it was not put on by George Edwardes at all. The famous "Guv'nor" died in 1915. His successor, Richard Evett, kept the name and beat all his old chief's records—and paid off his liabilities. "The Maid" ran for 1,352 performances.

No actress ever made so sudden and complete a conquest of Manchester as did José Collins that night. Youth, a voice described by the EVENING CHRONICLE as "glorious," and the perfect part rocketed her to fame.

She was the daughter of Lottie ("Ta-ra-ra-boom-de-ay") Collins, and she was born in Manchester. Most of the great Daly's achievements were. In Manchester, Gertie Millar, Lily Elsie and George Graves first went on the stage; in it were born Hayden Coffin and Joseph Harker, prince of musical comedy scene painters. Even "A Bachelor Gay," greatest hit among "The Maid's" songs, was written in the city—in the Midland Hotel.

FROM the launching of "The Dollar Princess" in 1908 most George Edwardes premières were in Manchester. The triumph of "The Maid of the Mountains" confirmed his posthumous domination. "A South-

José Collins at the peak of her fame as Teresa in " The Maid of the Mountains "

ern Maid," "The Lady of the Rose," "Sybil," "Katja the Dancer," and many more, all started their careers at the Prince's. Refreshed by Lancashire voices—including that of Accrington-born Derek Oldham—the Daly's tradition continued unbroken until the mid-1920's.

What was the secret? In an interview given to the EVENING CHRONICLE in his prime "The Guv'nor" answered: "England is the home of musical comedy. The sense of beauty and prettiness is developed on the English stage in a far higher degree than in the continental theatre."

For 20 years Manchester felt itself to be ahead of Paris or Vienna. But can reliance on prettiness and repetition of a formula make either a woman or a branch of entertainment everlastingly charming? It seems likely that even if the Prince's-Daly's recipe had not fallen into the hands of the Lancashire millionaire-gambler, Jimmy White, musical comedy would still have suffered decline.

George Edwardes the famous "Guv'nor"

"No Finer Feat..."

THE English celebrate their heroic failures in war rather than their victories. Among Northerners Gallipoli and the Somme are the best remembered battles of the First World War.

In the Somme, as Haig said, "Manchester was nobly represented." The 30th and 7th Divisions captured Montauban and Mametz in one of the most bitterly contested battles the world has ever seen. And after that came Bazentin, High Wood and Ginchy—not forgetting the part played by the Cheshires at Thiepval and Rawlinson's pride in their courage at Delville Wood.

But the sprawling, murderous Battle of the Somme, which cost 425,000 British casualties, lacks in historical retrospect the sharp outline of the assault on the precipitous peninsula of Gallipoli.

WHEN Xerxes crossed the Hellespont 2,500 years earlier, his Persians had a bridge of boats. In 1915 our men had only open boats from which to attack an entrenched enemy. No wonder a wave of emotion swept over Sir Ian Hamilton as he watched the scene. When he saw the Manchester Brigade disembarking at Achi Baba he thought :

"Here are the best the country can produce, the hope of the progress of the British ideal in the world, and half of them are going to swap lives with the Turks, whose relative value to the well-being of humanity is to their's as is a locust to a honey bee."

At "W" Beach, Cape Helles, the Lancashire Fusiliers "hurled themselves ashore and, fired at from right, left and centre, commenced hacking their way through the wire. A long line was at once mown down . . ."

Hamilton's final verdict on the assault will never be forgotten by Lancashire soldiers. It was this : "No finer feat of arms has ever been achieved by the British soldier or any other soldier."

Home Front, 1917

WHEN King George V toured Northern munition works in 1917 he was cheered by strikers. In Trafford Park, where he "clocked-on," he talked to one man who said that the employees at his works were the first to strike and the first to return.

It was a picturesque episode but not typical. At most times in the First World War a visitor would have found the North working as hard for victory as it did 25 years later. Women, wearing the knickerbockers of "lady students" learning to grow food, or the overalls of the war factory, did splendid work.

There was the usual wartime increase in juvenile crime and a rise in drunkenness among women. For the first time the police began to worry about treating and "red-biddy," a poisonous concoction which appeared about this period. Accordingly attempts were made to ban free snacks in bars, treating and even films about cabarets and night life.

SOME of the moral malaise was due to attempts to escape from and forget the load of grief imposed by the war which, in one sense, was harder than any Britain has ever fought. Slaughter at the fronts was terrible ; there were few people who did not lose a relative.

Grief was lifting in September, 1918, when Mr. Lloyd George visited Manchester to receive the Freedom of the City of his birth. "The worst is over," he cried, adding, in words which made an EVENING CHRONICLE headline : "There is not a crack in the joy bells ringing in our hearts."

Two months later all was quiet on the Western Front. The war was over.

The Old World turned out in solemn panoply of robe and uniform to welcome the spokesman of the New World when President Woodrow Wilson arrived in Manchester, December 30th, 1918. Front row (left to right) : Sir Robert Peacock, President Wilson, The Lord Mayor (Alderman J. Makeague) and Town Clerk (Mr. Thomas Hudson). Behind : Sir Daniel McCabe (wearing glasses) and Superintendent A. A. Lewis (with moustache)

"Sober, friendly Counsel"

"EVERYTHING for which America fought has been accomplished," wrote President Woodrow Wilson on November 11th, 1918. Six weeks later he was in England travelling from Carlisle to Manchester.

At that time Wilson seemed to be the arbiter of the world. Lancashire, which had just gone practically solid for the Lloyd George Coalition, did not clearly appreciate the significance of the fact that the U.S.A. had also had an election and that from now on the Democrat President would face a Republican Congress.

He was on his way to Paris to " establish just democracy throughout the world," by offering it " sober, friendly counsel." But what if people will not listen ? At the very moment of his arrival in Manchester friction broke out. Salford was resentful at being brusquely denied by Manchester the opportunity of presenting a resolution of welcome to the President. It was a miniature illustration of the jealousies he was to encounter at Versailles.

But these—and the arterio-sclerosis which was first to cripple and then kill Wilson— were still a little way ahead. However roughly Manchester treated Salford it could not have done more for its guest. The city council out-hustled America. It held a 90 seconds' meeting—the shortest on record— to appoint him a Freeman of the City.

After lunch the President went to the Royal Exchange, which promptly set aside its rule that no public speeches might be made on the floor. Officially this was because he was both a Freeman of Manchester and a native of the one of the Cotton States. But who can doubt that the real reason was that this was Woodrow Wilson, the man who was going to re-mould the world ?

Boom

For 14 months in 1919 and 1920 there was in Lancashire a boom the like of which had never been known before and, it is to be hoped, will never be known again.

At the end of the First World War a threadbare world began a wild scramble for goods, goods at any price. Cotton rose to three and a half times its normal value; the value of cotton goods exported soared to £316 millions (more than three times the 1913 figure) and whereas mill earnings before the war averaged $7\frac{1}{4}$ per cent they now rocketed to 40 per cent.

The pull of these figures was magnetic. Between May, 1919, and June, 1920, about 200 Lancashire mills changed hands, mostly at extravagant prices based on the high earnings of the boom period. The mills were promptly refloated and recapitalized. One hundred and eighty of these mills had, before recapitalization, a paid-up capital of £9,000,000. They were sold during the boom for £46,684,439, new shares being issued in exchange at the extent of £50,000,000 in £1 shares, usually 10s. paid, giving a capital of £25,000,000.

The boom began when the Pine Mill, Oldham, with 121,492 mule spindles and a comparatively small capital of £35,000 (1,000 £35 shares) was turned over at £135 a share, making a total of £135,000, and refloated with a capital of £120,000 in £1 fully-paid shares.

This was only a modest beginning. What happened later can be gauged from the fact that during the boom one leading man received from allotment of shares in 12 companies £3,241,948, with a net profit of over £1,000,000 in cash. Shareholders in eight companies with a total of 142,987 shares of £5 each received £2,186,877, while those who bought the shares and mills received £3,114,403, giving a profit of £927,526.

The boom stirred Lancashire as it had never been stirred before. Groups of promoters, chiefly mill directors and managers with a garnishing of " men of straw," came into being. Then clever London financiers took a hand, many of them selling at the first opportunity and taking their profits.

Among those attracted to the Lancashire jam-pot was E. T. Hooley, whose sensational bankruptcy in 1898 is recorded earlier in this book. He took a suite at the Midland Hotel, Manchester, and, in his own words, " lavish entertainment, unlimited lunches, champagne and cigars were the order of the day."

The boom was now at its peak. Every flotation attracted new speculators, at auction sales of shares the halls were not big enough to hold the bidders, and " paper " fortunes were made overnight.

Here is a typical case—and the sequel. The manager of a mill singled out for turning over was given 1,000 shares in the company which was sold for about ten times its value. His personal share when reflotation was complete was £10,000. Other deals followed, and within a few months this man had £150,000 within his grasp. But as he received most of his profits in shares, and also failed to cash in, his fortune vanished in a night when the slump came. He was left with a huge weight of uncalled capital, which broke him, as it broke many others, and he was paying off calls on his holdings for years.

The great bubble burst in the middle of 1920 and in the ensuing slump most of the £25,000,000 capital of the 180 mills was lost. There began a run of calls on unpaid capital, which likewise disappeared. Followed further calls which could not be met. Deeds of arrangement, not champagne lunches, were now the order of the day.

The banks, without whose support the bubble could never have become so fantastically inflated, suffered heavily. So did hosts of small loan investors, spinners and weavers who had placed their life savings in the mills in which they worked.

The last chapter was, for the future industrial health of Lancashire and Britain, worst of all. Mill after mill was offered for sale, but found no buyer except at scrap prices, and much of the machinery was carted away to be shipped to Lancashire's competitors.

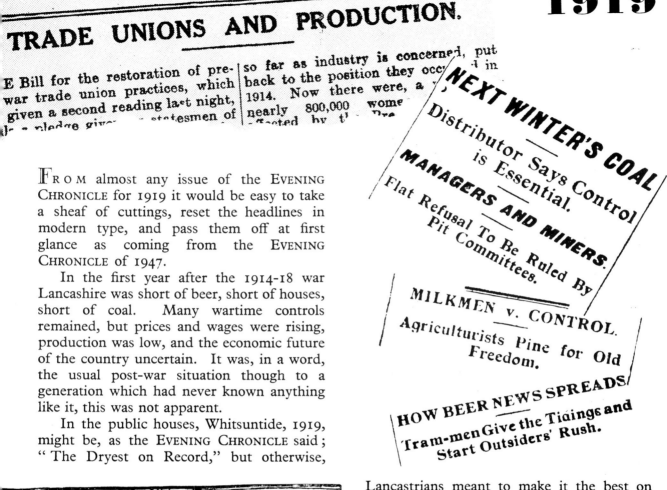

TRADE UNIONS AND PRODUCTION.

E Bill for the restoration of pre-war trade union practices, which given a second reading last night, ... pledge give... statesmen of so far as industry is concerned, put back to the position they occu...d in 1914. Now there were, a ... nearly 800,000 women ... ...ted by t'...

FROM almost any issue of the EVENING CHRONICLE for 1919 it would be easy to take a sheaf of cuttings, reset the headlines in modern type, and pass them off at first glance as coming from the EVENING CHRONICLE of 1947.

In the first year after the 1914-18 war Lancashire was short of beer, short of houses, short of coal. Many wartime controls remained, but prices and wages were rising, production was low, and the economic future of the country uncertain. It was, in a word, the usual post-war situation though to a generation which had never known anything like it, this was not apparent.

In the public houses, Whitsuntide, 1919, might be, as the EVENING CHRONICLE said; "The Dryest on Record," but otherwise,

NEXT WINTER'S COAL
Distributor Says Control is Essential.

MANAGERS AND MINERS.
Flat Refusal To Be Ruled By Pit Committees.

MILKMEN v. CONTROL.
Agriculturists Pine for Old Freedom.

HOW BEER NEWS SPREADS
Tram-men Give the Tidings and Start Outsiders' Rush.

Lancastrians meant to make it the best on record. It was a summer of storming good holidays, victory parades and parties.

DURING the next two years economic slump tarnished the glamour of "Reconstruction," while leaving the need for it more urgent than ever. There was much talk about the Government's "ruinous expenditure" and the cloud of "unproductive bureaucrats." Baffled Conservative Chancellors were baited no less than hapless Liberals, like Mr. Addison, who had been given the job of finding 500,000 houses.

The houses did not appear and to say "I'm living in Addison Road," became a synonym for being homeless. Manchester, who had talked of building 6,750 houses a year, erected only 97 by the end of 1920. A primitive "squatting" movement appeared.

"The position John Redmond holds in England to-day." This was the caption of an *Evening Chronicle* cartoon on the Irish problem which was in eruption from 1912 to 1922

It was pioneered by Alderman E. J. Hart who, with a fellow city councillor, broke into a house in Moss Side, Manchester, and installed in it an ex-Service-man and his family.

WHEN Stanley Houghton made the heroine of " Hindle Wakes " live at " No. 137, Burnley Road . . . a house rented at about 7s. 6d. a week," he accurately described pre-war standards. In 1920 a new house cost £1,000 and the economic rent, at the high rate of interest then prevailing, was 30s. a week. Not until 1923, the fifth year after the war, was there much building in Lancashire.

By that time the North-West, in addition to grappling with its own cotton trade slump, had been caught up in two big post-war national storms—the Sinn Fein troubles and the great coal strike of 1921.

Liverpool and Manchester were centres of Irish agitation and in 1920 a rising was planned to take place simultaneously in both cities. The plot was detected in time, but outrages continued until, in April, 1921, the police raided a club in Hulme which they discovered was both an arsenal and the headquarters where the outrages were planned. Shots rang out and one man fell dead. At the next Assizes 16 men were sent to penal servitude, but amnestied later.

At this period Lord Derby made his famous trip to Dublin where he met some of the Irish leaders. He travelled incognito as " Mr. Edwards." Tradition says he also went disguised, but he himself pooh-poohed the story, claiming that the " disguise " was no more than a pair of heavy tortoiseshell glasses.

" Squatters " in 1920 ! Alderman E. J. Hart, with screwdriver, and Councillor Hales, armed with a hammer, after seizing an empty house in Manchester

THE coal strike of the same year was a grim by - product of the prevailing industrial depression and of the Coalition Government's attempt to disengage itself from its wartime commitments. Under State control the cost of producing coal was now 6s. more than the selling price. The mines were costing the taxpayer £5,000,000 a month and were considered bankrupt.

When the industry was decontrolled the owners announced wage cuts of up to 40 per cent, whereupon the miners sought a great Triple Alliance strike in coal, railways and general transport.

In the end miners and owners were left to fight it out, which they did for the unprecedented term of 13 weeks. In the North-West the strike was endured with surprising indifference by the public. A fine summer helped to encourage this attitude, but probably the chief explanation was that the average man was tired of arguing about economic problems which he felt unable to cure. Besides, as we shall see, a new decade was beginning to offer him new diversions and new interests.

ATLANTIC FLIGHT
Start To-day by Captain Alcock?
MANCHESTER PILOT.
Admiralty Report of Unfavourable Weather.
A wireless message from Cape Race says that the Vickers-Vimy machine leaves St. John's, Newfoundland, to-day.—Wireless Press.

In the summer of 1919 the public was stirred by reports of attempts to fly the Atlantic. Few believed they would succeed. But in June the unexpected happened

The first Transatlantic aircraft in flight and, on right, its crew Alcock and Brown

Alcock and Brown

" Where are you from ? "
" St. John's, Newfoundland."

This answer, given by two rather dazed airmen to the staff at the Clifton Wireless Station, in the far west of Ireland, on June 15th, 1919, raised a hearty laugh. The wireless men, who had rushed to the plane, whose nose was now buried in a bog, were incredulous, facetious.

In this way ended the first non-stop crossing of the Atlantic by John Alcock and Arthur Whitten Brown. Flying an adapted Vickers-Vimy Rolls Royce, they set out on Saturday, June 14th, and completed the trip in 16 hours 12 minutes.

Soon the genuineness of their story became manifest, and within three days they had been given an almost royal reception in London and knighted by the King.

Both were Manchester men. Alcock, whose father worked for the Evening Chronicle, lived in Fallowfield, and Brown was from Chorlton. The first congratulatory wire to reach Alcock's father was from Sir Edward Hulton, and Sir Harry Brittain wired the Lord Mayor of Manchester : " Where Manchester has flown to-day let the rest of the world try and follow to-morrow."

Sir John Alcock's enjoyment of the honours accorded him by his native city and country was brief. While flying to Paris he was injured in a forced landing and died on December 18th, 1919. He was buried in Southern Cemetery, Manchester, where a headstone and model aeroplane commemorate his achievement.

Sir Arthur Whitten Brown, happily still alive, made his second Atlantic flight as recently as last year, crossing from London to New York in 9 hours 45 minutes in an 8,000 h.p. plane. His 1919 machine was of 750 h.p.

Were the Twenties Dirty?

THE 1920's are still too close to us to have acquired the patina of the picturesque. To some they are still " The Dirty Twenties " : others see them as years in which more new ideas were stirring than at any time since the Nineties.

What will not be disputed is that the Twenties, especially the early Twenties, worked overtime demolishing old assumptions. Iconoclasts held jamboree and debunking was the pastime of the day. Lytton Strachey is credited—or charged—with leading the onslaught. But whereas he exposed only the illustrious dead, a Lancashire man simultaneously debunked the illustrious living. Gerald Cumberland's " Set Down in Malice " —the accuracy of the title was never disputed —revealed a diabolical knack of baring its victims' weak spots. Naturally the book became both a model and a scandal.

THERE were a great many scandalized people about in the Twenties. In 1919 the hem of a skirt was six inches from the ground ; by 1925 it leaped to 16 inches— and stayed there. As if by some law of compensation, hats came down to nose level and faces smiled in perpetual shadow.

Waists disappeared and corsets threatened to follow suit ; heavy make-up and shorn hair, regarded as signs of doubtful morality in 1918, became normal. Shorter frocks meant less demand for Lancashire textiles and, as flesh-coloured rayon stockings neither looked, felt nor wore well with clogs, many mill girls began to wear shoes—often very bad ones.

Stern moralists saw in all this a reflection of the age's flight from " wholesome standards," particularly sex standards. Sex may, indeed, have been no more of an obsession than in other decades, but it was talked about a great deal more publicly. Risky jokes had a run in the music halls, and such horrified husbands as were candid enough to believe their own ears realized that those who laughed loudest were often women. Furthermore, the petting party, " companionate marriage," and other transatlantic innovations came in.

THE truth is that in the Twenties most new things came from America. In Edwardian times Lancashire could invent a world-capturing dance like the military two-step ; now all new dances came from the U.S.A. Thence also came Mah-jong, put-and-take, Mickey Mouse, Rudolph Valentino and other ephemeral crazes. It looked as if this really was going to be " The American Century."

A few of the importations proved more durable. Greyhound and speedway racing were pioneered in Lancashire,

" Skirts leaped . . . waists disappeared . . . hats came down . . ."

and it was a sign of the times that Blackpool's Pleasure Beach, which had consisted of a few roundabouts and swings in 1901, went on to beat the U.S.A. at its own game. The one indigenous lasting pastime which strode to the front at this period was rambling, especially in the Peak, the Lakes and North Wales.

ALL these are snapshots of the top layer of life in the Twenties. Beneath ran a stream of real idealism. Typical of it was the loving care lavished on the building of Liverpool Cathedral (consecrated 1924), and the first big-scale attempts to give industrial workers homes in which they might live pleasantly and with dignity. Wythenshawe, the talk of the world in the 1930's, was planned in the 1920's.

There was much activity in the Arts, notwithstanding the attempt to ridicule this through bracketing " highbrow " with " Victorian " as fashionable period terms of abuse. Under Sir Hamilton Harty, the Hallé Orchestra became once again the finest in England and, stirred by the brilliant, uneconomic example set by Sir Thomas Beecham, opera was presented in the provinces at a level unequalled before or since. William Walton, born at Oldham, was the outstanding young British composer of the period, and it was another Lancastrian—

Both famous for their ministrations in Manchester, the late Archbishop Temple is here seen on the occasion of his enthronement as Archbishop of Canterbury with the Dean of Canterbury, the Very Rev. Hewlett Johnson

known best by his back—who made the syncopated music of the time into more than a collection of bizarre noises. His name was Jack Hylton.

In literature a new generation of writers were springing up athwart the Pennines. They included J. B. Priestley, Louis Golding, Winifred Holtby, Phyllis Bentley and J. L. Hodson. In dialect literature, which is as Lancashire as an Eccles cake, Bills o' Jacks (Wm. Baron) and Sam Fitton died in the 1920's, but the elf-like Ammon Wrigley was still writing, and T. Thompson, of Bury, destined to win a wider audience than previous masters of dialect, was sharpening his pen.

From this dialect tradition sprang the mostly widely-known Lancastrian of the period. This was Gracie Fields, the one-time Rochdale mill lass. Cotton might languish, but Lancashire folk-humour proved readily exportable. Gracie gave it an almost world-wide currency.

GOTHIC, PLUS DOME—A suggested design for Liverpool Cathedral, published in 1901. It was not accepted

The Beginning of Radio

"This is 2ZY calling." These words, first broadcast regularly on November 15th, 1922, did not cause much stir—at first. Twenty-five years ago there were only 50,000 wireless listeners in Britain and, for the moment, Lancashire was absorbed in the results of the General Election which was putting Mr. Lloyd George out of power and Mr. Bonar Law in.

It was a Lancashire man, Sir Ambrose Fleming, who made

"The Butterfly on Wheel," first full-len drama ever broadcast production. Victor Sm (standing) directed the and Pat Ryan of the H provided the incide music . . . on a clarine

PLAUDITS FOR "CHRONICLE" RADIO EXHIBITION.

Keen Interest in Latest Developments:
The Woman's Point of View:
Attractive Concert Features.

By CRYSTAL. Amplion. The set is switched on and off
The great Wireless Exhibition by means of a push and pull switch.
organised by the *Evening Chronicle* Although tested in the Exhibition Hall,
and Provincial Exhibitions, Ltd., with practically surrounded by metalwork, the
loud-speaker reception was of consider-

By DETECTOR.
Many people would like to fit clocks
coupling instead of transformer, but
amidst the loss of amplification due to

broadcasting possible when he invented the thermionic valve, the Aladdin's lamp of radio. It was another Fleming—now Sir Arthur—who brought radio to the North.

Early in 1922 he constructed at Trafford Park an experimental transmitter for Metropolitan Vickers. By July, the tests were arousing the enthusiasm of wireless amateurs, one of whom wrote to the Press about the "extraordinary clarity" with which records of Caruso and music from Gilbert and Sullivan operas came over the air.

The broadcasters had enthusiasm, too, but no comfort. The studio was a cramped

Dan Godfrey, junr. sported a football jersey when conducting an early symphony concert in the indoor-tent studio

Before Radio. The first means of broadcasting " canned " music to crowds was through gramophone concerts in the parks. This one was held in Boggart Hole Clough, Manchester, in 1908

canvas cabin, built on a wooden framework, and littered with packing cases and primitive properties for making wild stabs at sound effects. At any moment listeners might be adjured : " Wait five minutes while we move the piano."

Into this cabin the performers, famous or otherwise, had to squeeze, and here, too, the " Kiddies' Corner "—forerunner of the Children's Hour—was played. Uncle Humpty Dumpty, kept from falling off the wall by Uncle Jumbo, was Mr. Kenneth Wright. He was in charge of the station, and Jumbo, for all his elephantine pretences, was named Nightingale.

Few artists foresaw the commercial possibilities of radio. Norman Long, who first broadcast in 1922, has left it on record that he did not, though after several appearances he did receive a cheque for " nominal expenses." It was for one guinea !

THE following year 2 ZY migrated to a warehouse in Dickenson Street, Manchester, and, in 1924, to Orme's Buildings, near the Irwell. In the former, the attic studio was reached by a cotton hoist ; in the latter, the singers warbled in a room below water level.

By this time the radio boom had arrived. You could buy a crystal set for 13s., and, if you were clever and knew all about cats' whiskers and the mysterious properties of galena, you might make one yourself for 3s.

Then, wearing earphones, you settled down to listen to Dan Godfrey, junior, or T. H. Morrison conducting the wireless band until Victor Smythe said " Good night, everybody." This he did so romantically that thousands of " flappers " wrote for his autograph.

In the late twenties and early thirties many old landmarks of Manchester disappeared and great modern buildings took their place. It was at that time that the home of the "Evening Chronicle" took its present form

Evening Chronicle

The twelve months starting in October, 1923, are pivotal in the history of the EVENING CHRONICLE. Ill-health compelled Sir Edward Hulton to sell his newspapers, and by spring 1924 they were under the control of Allied Newspapers, whose name was later changed to Kemsley Newspapers.

In Manchester the mid-1920's were a period of refreshment and enterprise after the black frost of war and its aftermath. Building went forward again. The Ship Canal, the Bleachers and Lewis's were all planning or erecting new homes, and in Withy Grove the old Chronicle Office was being replaced by a great new building destined to become the world's largest newspaper office.

The EVENING CHRONICLE, reduced to four pages in the war years, was now back to eight pages and ready to leap forward. New features were started. The first was Denys's "Northern Window." Hitherto the paper had carried general notes and London gossip. The "Northern Window" assumed, rightly, that the North-West had abundant material to provide its own talk of the day.

Simultaneously the paper began to cater energetically for the new radio public which was then springing up. "Crystal" and "Radidea" quickly became popular pen names, and, in October, 1924, the EVENING CHRONICLE promoted the biggest wireless

Through a Northern Window By Denys

exhibition held in Britain up to that time. Thereafter radio exhibitions, sponsored by the paper and opened by celebrities like Lord Reith, Lord Gainford, Mrs. Philip (later Viscountess) Snowden, and Professor W. L. Bragg, were held annually.

By the end of 1924 the EVENING CHRONICLE was, on some days, 12 pages in size. But that was only a beginning. By the early Thirties issues of 20 and even 24 pages were normal weekly events. News was brought to the front page in 1929, features were developed and scores of new activities promoted.

Contests of all kinds from dressmaking and gardening to table tennis, bowls and angling were very popular. Ballots were held on matters of public opinion, and the results sometimes make quaint reading to-day. For instance, a poll taken in 1929 on the relative popularity of silent and talking films gave a heavy majority for the " silents." Talkies had yet to show what they could do.

Among the contributors to the *Chronicle* Cinderella Club's Doll Show in 1931 was Gracie Fields, and Mr. Jesse Hewitt, Managing Director of the Palace Theatre, Manchester, received her gift on behalf of the Club. Mr. Hewitt and the *Evening Chronicle* are almost "twins." He celebrated his Jubilee of service at the Manchester Palace in February, 1947. He started there as office boy

For the benefit of readers at Wembley for the Manchester City v. Portsmouth Cup Final, in 1934, the *Evening Chronicle*, printed in Manchester, was flown to London and sold on the streets there

A BIRTHDAY CLUB was started for children who, along with their fathers, flocked to "Chronicle" exhibitions of "Models and Marvels," while their mothers inspected "Homes and Fashions" exhibitions opened by well known women like Marie Tempest and Lady Maureen Stanley.

Other strokes of enterprise included, at one extreme, the bringing to Manchester of Maurice Chevalier in the first days of his international popularity (1930), and the use well in advance of competitors of the telephoto process and of the aeroplane. By 1934, when Manchester City won the F. A. Cup, Northerners who went to Wembley could buy the EVENING CHRONICLE in London little over two hours after the match.

AMID these developments a traditional activity of the paper was steadily cherished. This was the running of the Chronicle Cinderella Club. It grew out of Robert Blatchford's studies of 19th century poverty in Manchester, and was devoted to the brightening of poor children's lives by giving them Christmas treats and seaside holidays.

The Club's Christmas Doll Show, to which King George V and Queen Mary, as well as famous Lancastrians like Lord Derby, made gifts; attracted thousands of visitors. It also raised large sums for the children, as did the annual Cinderella Concert at the old Free Trade Hall. This concert was the Lancashire equivalent of a London Command Performance. In 1939 the Club was transformed into a War Fund, which, under the chairmanship of Lady Helen Berry, was affiliated to Viscountess Kemsley's *Daily Sketch* War Fund. In six years over £69,000 was raised to provide comforts for the Services.

Ship Canal House and the Midland Bank building, the giants of King Street, dwarfing their elders

Cricket

By A. W. LEDBROOKE

ARTHUR MOLD

On May 10th, 1897, Mold bowled out Derbyshire for a paltry score. It was the first day of a new cricket season, as bleak as only an English May can be after the rich promise of April. But the start of Lancashire's season could not have been more happily timed to coincide with the birth of the new evening paper.

The history of club and newspaper became interwoven through the years from that summer, when Lancashire won their first clear-cut championship since 1881, and the EVENING CHRONICLE set a fashion for other newspapers. This was to send a representative not only to home, but to away matches, thus maintaining a continuity of interest and an independence of judgment annoying at first to A. N. Hornby, the Lancashire skipper, but eventually of untold benefit to the game.

From 1897 onwards great cricketers adorned the Lancashire side right up to last autumn when Washbrook, Ikin and Pollard sailed with the M.C.C. team to Australia. A whole volume—and a long one—could be written of cricket in the county. Here we can only recall some shining names and hope that to cricket lovers they will serve as a reminder of happy days in the sun.

How they illuminate and crowd the pages of *Wisden*! MacLaren, aristocrat of the crease and cleverest of captains, has a place of his own in Test and county cricket. Ranged behind him come Johnny and Ernest Tyldesley, Albert Ward, Johnny Briggs, Reggie Spooner, and the Westhoughton Tyldesleys. Then there crowd upon the turf the double internationals, Sharp and Makepeace ; Cook, Heap, Dean and Cuttell ; the Australian MacDonald ; Walter Brearley, Jimmy and Charlie Hallows, George Duckworth, Eddie Paynter, Peter Eckersley and Jack Iddon.

The county championship was won again in 1904. Then came a long interval until three successive wins from 1926 onwards. A spell of Yorkshire supremacy followed, but Lancashire broke the White Rose monopoly with further championships in 1930 and 1934.

Lancashire cricket means much more than just Old Trafford. Club and league cricket flourishes side by side and it was here, while he was playing with Rishton, that the matchless brilliance of Sydney Barnes was revealed. After his first trip to Australia, he played two full seasons with Lancashire and then returned to league cricket, emerging occasionally to scatter destruction among the finest Test match batsmen of Australia and South Africa.

Old Trafford's Test matches have yielded their dramatic stories, from Tate's missed catch and a three-runs win for Australia in 1902 to O'Reilly's three wickets in four balls in 1934. And it must be whispered that twice a Test match due to start has been completely washed out.

Cricket abounds with humour as well as drama and just one story, linking game with newspaper, may be told. In the 1900's a young journalist went to Warrington to report a club game, taking with him, as was the custom of the time, his basket of pigeons to relay the scores back to the office. Walter Brearley, who was playing in the match, boisterously greeted the reporter with : " Hello, Bob ; what have you got in that basket ? " . . . *and lifted the lid* !

The reporter was Bob Gowanlock, who later on, became " Red Rose " of the EVENING CHRONICLE, and followed the succession of J. J. Bentley, J. A. H. Catton, Roy Young and A. R. Booth.

WHO CAN MATCH THEM ?   Here, with a background of Old Trafford during a Test match, are a few of the stars of cricket :
1, A. N. Hornby ; 2, Archie MacLaren ; 3, '' Reggie '' Spooner ; 4, J. T. Tyldesley ; 5, Jack Sharp ; 6, Syd Barnes ; 7, The bowling hand of Barnes ; 8, R. Tyldesley ; 9, George (Ow-zat) Duckworth and 10—We co-opt him as a Lancashireman, the famous West Indian, Learie Constantine

8

9

10

COAL CLOUD ON THE POLITICAL HORIZON

IS COUNTRY BEING VICTIMISED ?

Alleged Attempt to Bluff the Premier

GASHED MAN IN CITY KITCHEN

Woman Remanded on Grave Charge.

MIDNIGHT DRAMA

GENTLE PUSH FOR MAN ON SPOUT.

Sisters Screams in the Night.

EX-NAVY MAN FINED

From Our Own Correspondent.

EASTER SHOWS A SUMMER FRILL.

Hotter To-day Than Yesterday.

RUSH TO THE OPEN.

CITY HOUSES ON NEW SYSTEM.

Concrete Interiors and No Plasterers.

SPEEDING-UP PLAN

LOVER W NOT TU

Surprise and N

CHARGE O

General Strike

THE 9,000th issue of the EVENING CHRONICLE was the smallest on record. It was a single sheet of paper 14 ins. by eight, containing about 300 words—and it appeared two days late.

It should have been published on May 4th, 1926, and the reason why it did not appear was the outbreak of the ten days' General Strike of 2,700,000 workers.

The General Strike was really a continuation and culmination of the troubles which bred the coal strike of 1921. The miners won increased wages in 1924, but a slump set in and the owners gave notice to reduce wages. The Government offered a temporary subsidy and set up a Royal Commission, one of whose members was Mr. Kenneth Lee, of Manchester. Among other things they recommended a reduction of mining wages " on a temporary basis." This the miners refused. Organized labour was sympathetic and, when the subsidy ended, a General Strike was called on May 4th.

ON that Tuesday morning hardly any passenger trains ran, trams were at a standstill and few newspapers appeared. In theory, a revolutionary situation existed, and nervous people thought that military protection would be needed. But the strikers, far from manning barricades, were mostly busy on their allotments, crowding cinemas, and watching or playing cricket.

It is probably true that the English instinct for sport and play did as much as patriotism, let alone class consciousness, to beat the

Manchester transport workers demonstrating in Albert Square, Manchester, during the General Strike. Note the White Star Building in course of erection

strike. Men who had longed from childhood to drive an engine flocked forward as volunteers and, in its miniature edition of May 7th, the EVENING CHRONICLE reported that 500 L.M.S. trains were running. In all 2,400 trains ran that day.

Public appetite for news of the strike had to be fed on improvised rations. At first large bills were placed in the CHRONICLE office window, while a mutagraph flashed the latest news " snaps " in Piccadilly. Then little multigraph editions of the paper were issued and bought eagerly.

ON May 12th the T.U.C. called on Mr. Baldwin and said : " We are here to-day, sir, to say that this General Strike is to be terminated forthwith." By the 14th work was being resumed and next day Manchester newspapers re-appeared in their normal dress.

But the miners refused to give ·in. Although as early as May 27th the EVENING CHRONICLE reported great distress among their families in parts of Lancashire, the men hung on grimly. Led by sturdy cloth-capped Herbert Smith and A. J. Cook, an impassioned orator, they stayed out of the pits all summer. By September there was a drift back to the mines in the North-West. In the end, which came in late November, the miners had to accept district settlements.

The number of working days lost in Britain in 1926 was 162,230,000—double the number recorded in any year before or since. Of these, only 15,000,000 days were accounted for by the General Strike.

MANCHESTER EVENING CHRONICLE

No. 9,000 (Registered as a Newspaper) Thurs, May 6th. 1926. 1

GENERAL STRIKE SITUATION.

There was no material change in the strike situation to-day. The railway companies reported slightly improved services. A new development was reported with reference to the activities of T.U.C. Mr. C.T. Cramp, the Industrial Secretary of the N.U.R., issued instructions to the effect that N.U.R. and Transport men should not handle foodstuffs.

TRAMS & TRAINS.

Liverpool reported 70% of normal tram service resumed. Workers returning to work in large numbers. Hastings tram service resumed on several routes to-day. Independent omnibus proprietors running in London. Policeman on front of each 'bus. They are not meeting with any interference. The L & N.E.R. reported that they had operated yesterday 281 trains, which ran 8.508 miles. More trains are reported leaving London for provinces. The Southern Railway ran 334 trains, including service to and from Continent. Trains left Manchester for London at 9.30 and 12 noon to day.

INDUSTRIAL MOVEMENTS.

Workmen are returning to work in various centres, but not in large numbers. On the other hand, men have left work at several places. Five hundred Royal Aircraftsmen, who are also trade unionists, ceased work at Farnborough last night. Increasing number of men resuming work in L.M.S. Railway Company's Works at Wolverhampton. Five hundred clerks have joined strikers at Cardiff. Messrs. Whitehead's, who have large steelworks at Newport (Mon.) report that their works have restarted, 95% of workmen having returned.

STRIKE DISTURBANCES.

There were rowdy scenes near Elephant Castle, South London, to-day. A 'bus was set on fire after passengers, driver, and conductor had been ordered off. Flames were put out by firemen. Extra police drafted into neighbourhood. At Edinburgh a crowd of several thousand came into conflict with police, at whom bottles and stones were thrown. Five constables and a number of civilians are in hospital. Five arrests were made.

Mr. SAKLATVALA.

Mr. Saklatvala M.P. at Bow-street to day refused to be bound over in sureties to keep peace and elected to go to prison for two months in the second division.

CRICKET.

Yorks. 176. 50 for 1. Cambridge U. 176 Glamorgan v Surrey 220 for 6. Worcester 194 Lancs. 51 for 1. Australians v Essex 276 for 3.
Printed and Published by ALLIED NEWSPAPERS LTD., Withy Grove, Manchester.

The 9,000th Issue

Birtwistle "Millions"

EVERY mayoress of Colne wears a diamond of exceptional beauty. It is held in trust by the Town Council and is a visible reminder that in April, 1948, the people of Colne will come into a fortune of about £150,000.

The original owner of both the diamond and the fortune was Peter Birtwistle, of Toronto, who died on April 19th, 1927, aged 85. Sixty years earlier he left his native Colne to seek his fortune in Canada. In old age his thoughts turned back to the steep, cobbled streets of Colne and the weavers and working folk he had known in his youth.

In 1917 he notified Colne Corporation that he intended leaving a big sum to the town. A Peter Birtwistle Trust was set up under which his invested fortune was to accumulate for 21 years after his death.

Next year the funds are to be paid to the Corporation of Colne to be used " for the benefit of the aged and deserving poor of the town without restriction of any kind, in such manner as shall be deemed prudent to the Council."

Peacetime "Blackout"

FOR the only time in 200 years, hundreds of thousands of Northerners struggled for " a place *out* of the Sun " on June 29th, 1927.

The reason was that at 6-25 a.m. a total eclipse of the Sun was visible in England for the first time since 1725. The track of totality, 30 miles wide, entered Britain at Criccieth, passing through Southport, Stonyhurst and Settle. Parties of astronomers invaded Lancashire and Yorkshire to observe and photograph the spectacle.

The railway companies did not at first appreciate the enormous interest aroused, but in the end they ran excursions from all parts of Britain to Lancashire and Pennines. Return fare from London was 17s.

THE sky was cloudy, but thousands of people rose in the middle of the night and rode or walked to the totality zone in the hope of seeing the incandescent, radiant glow of the Sun's corona, visible to the naked eye only during full eclipse.

At Settle and Giggleswick, where the Greenwich Observatory party set up their instruments, 100,000 people assembled. At Blackpool the eclipse was welcomed, after a night of revelry, by crowds dancing the Charleston.

Compared with the astronomers' equipment most of the apparatus seen at Giggleswick was elementary—just bits of smoked glass

Over much of Lancashire the eclipse was a game of hide and seek between sun and cloud. But at Giggleswick the sky cleared for the vital 24 seconds, and the corona shone in fleeting glory.

" Wonderful ! Wonderful ! " cried Sir Frank Dyson, Astronomer Royal, to the EVENING CHRONICLE reporter. "A glorious eclipse."

They Called Him Jimmy

FORTY years ago a laughable story was going the rounds. The then Duke of Devonshire entertained his tenants to a banquet in a Matlock swimming bath which had been covered over for the occasion. Part of the floor gave way and Duke and guests fell into the bath.

This misadventure might have served as both a parable and a prediction, for the man who covered the bath for the Duke was James White, of Rochdale. A dozen years later his entertainments eclipsed any ducal spread. He was reputed to be worth £4,000,000. Then, in June, 1927, the floor of his fortunes collapsed, and he died tragically.

JIMMY WHITE, born in Half Moon Yard, Rochdale, started in the mill as a doffer at the age of ten. Later he worked as a bricklayer, bought a circus for £100, and went to seek his fortune in South Africa. But conditions had changed on the Rand since the early days of Barny Barnato and Rhodes, and Jimmy White had to work his passage back to England and then tramp home to Rochdale.

He laid more bricks, speculated in property, went bankrupt and, after declaring he would pay 20s. in the £—a promise faithfully kept—he said : " In Rochdale they are too timid. They fight shy of big things."

He borrowed £200, went to London, installed himself in a very good hotel, and began operations. With little education, and less capital, but armed with abundant native wit and audacity, he rapidly came to the front, startling England in 1913 by joining Sir Joseph Beecham to buy the Covent Garden Estate for £3,000,000. He was, in short, Arnold Bennett's " The Card " to the life.

He bought anything and everything, including Daly's Theatre and the Wembley Exhibition site ; he developed Dunlops and, to the resentment of some manufacturers, brought London finance into the cotton trade in a big way. In one year he put through transactions amounting to £50,000,000. Then, in the mid-1920's, his affairs became involved and, finding himself unable to raise £900,000 for which he was liable, he drove to his country house near Swindon and took poison.

AT the height of his prosperity Jimmy White was the most extravagant, most generous man alive. He patronized the ring, owned racehorses, and backed fantastically— as much as £100,000 a bet. It was typical of him that when he entertained his boyhood working men friends each had three bottles of champagne, and benedictine was drunk from tumblers. It is said that he never forgot a kindness ; it is a fact that he put many people on the way to fame and fortune and had a warm heart for Rochdale.

A vast mass of stories, partly myth, partly truth, clustered around his exploits. They show him as a humorous gambler rather than as anything worse. Even his critics had a soft spot for him. Exactly 30 years before his death, the EVENING CHRONICLE, commenting on the suicide of Barny Barnato, said : " Let there be no cant about Barnato. There were many worse." In 1927, Lancashire said much the same about Jimmy White.

en Jimmy White died he left the remarkable collection
cing trophies seen on the opposite page. Collected between
and 1925, they include : The Jockey Club Cup (1919)
by Gay Lord ; Royal Hunt Cup (1919), Irish Elegance ;
dwood Cup (1925), Cloudbank ; Newbury Cup (1922),
sman ; Liverpool Spring Cup (1923), Clochnaleen ; and the
chester Gold Cup (1922) won by North Waltham. Of gold
silver, they weighed 1,246 ozs.

An early home of "animated pictures." The old St. James's Hall, Oxford Street, Manchester

The Cinema

November 14th, 1928, is an historic date in this history of entertainment in Britain. On that day the New Oxford Cinema, Manchester, presented the first complete " talkie " programme shown outside America. It was a 12-reel film of " Uncle Tom's Cabin " with an " all-recorded background."

Few foresaw the completeness of the coming revolution any more than Lancashire realized the possibilities inherent in " living pictures " when they were first shown with the original Lumiere Cinematographe at the Free Trade Hall on May 18th, 1896.

That was just a year before the birth of the EVENING CHRONICLE, whose fifty years reflects in its columns what is, for all practical purposes, the entire growth of the cinema. In 1897, living pictures were already rivalling —though as novelties only—artists like Little Tich and Vesta Tilley at the Manchester

Palace, and the Edison Biograph was included in the programme at the old Comedy with such " shorts " as " Persimmon Winning the Derby," " The Diamond Jubilee," and the naively-titled " Scenes of an Engineer Working."

For the next few years primitive news reels were edging their way into the programmes of most music halls or running as added attractions on Lancashire fairgrounds, where barrel-organs blared to drown the noises made by the projecting machines.

By the turn of the century the Great St. James's Hall (the C.P.A. Building now stands on the site) and the Free Trade Hall were running neck and neck for the right to be regarded as the home of animated pictures in Manchester. While the Free Trade Hall delved into the mysteries of sound by wedding a gramophone and the cinematograph for a version of "The Village Blacksmith," the St. James's was boasting that 1,250,000 people had attended its 18-weeks' season of Edison's "world-famed animated pictures." More than 200 films had been shown, including "The Lord Mayor of London's visit to Manchester," "Dumont's Aerial Ship" and "The Funeral of the Empress Frederick." Prices ranged from 6d. to 3s.—with two military bands thrown in.

Six years later Lancashire saw its first coloured films, each separate "frame" hand-tinted with infinite patience. The days of imagination and adventure had arrived. "Hales' Tours of the World," for which patrons paid coppers to watch inside imitation railway carriages, rocked for the occasion, were being shown at White City. Also, in a converted hall in Moss Side, another show-man was rolling pellets in an empty film-can to impart "sea effects" to a screening of "Christopher Columbus."

"THE PICTURES," as they were coming to be called, were capturing popular imagination. There was a rush to adapt suitable halls by installing seating, a projecting box in the middle of the room, and a white-washed screen. With cheerful disdain for public safety, the illuminant for the projector was provided by a naked jet of coal gas mixed with oxygen which made white-hot a cylindrical block—a relic of the Victorian magic lantern.

Which was the first regular cinema in Manchester is a matter of debate. The Bijou, Hulme, the New Oxford and the "picture palace" at the Alhambra, Openshaw, all opened about 1907. In the same year the Colosseum was opened as Blackpool's first regular cinema. The film was "The Life of Christ."

BY 1914 the cinema had penetrated to even the smallest towns, meeting with some sales resistance on the journey. Gifts of oranges or chocolate bars were made to tempt young patrons, and at one Lancashire cinema jam-jars instead of cash were accepted as the price of admission !

In the early 1920's there was, together with the great advance in the quality of silent

In the early part of the century the arrival of great sailing ships provided a special thrill for holiday makers on the beach at Fleetwood

In matters concerning the " noble art " Lancashire claims many champions and that champion of champions, Lord Lonsdale (inset). The boxers are that famous trio, Jock McAvoy, British Light Heavyweight Champion, 1937-38, and undefeated British Middleweight Champion since 1933. Jackie Brown, British Flyweight Champion, 1929-30, 1931-35, European Flyweight Champion 1931-35, World Flyweight Champion 1932-35. Johnny King, British Bantamweight Champion 1932-34 and 1935-47

films, a partial return to the old mixture of cinema and variety. Orchestras were installed, and sometimes famous artistes provided musical or dramatic interludes. The divine Sarah Bernhardt made her last appearance in Manchester as an interlude at the Gaiety. She was engaged by Ludwig Blattner who exerted much influence during this phase of mixing films with other attractions.

ALL this ended abruptly in 1929 with the arrival of the first talkies. Orchestras were now deemed superfluous ; hundreds of instrumentalists were thrown out of work. Cinema-variety wavered and then tottered. The wedding of sound and sight meant that the cinema could supply anything.

For a few months the marriage was not without friction. Technically, recording and equipment were far from perfect. Faults rasped out like rifle-shots. Indeed, when Mr. Gordon Smith, the enterprising manager of the New Oxford, showed a film of a concert party, supposedly performing behind the front in the First World War, he told audiences that the noises were " machine-guns firing up the line." They departed satisfied, marvelling at the new wonder.

To-day there are 150 cinemas in the Manchester and Salford district, and the neighbourhood has provided two outstanding screen stars of the past decade—Robert Donat and Wendy Hiller. Finally, Manchester is the first city to produce its own civic film, " A City Speaks."

T' Flat-Iron

SALFORD's Flat-Iron Market, well-known landmark of which the city was never proud, closed down in June, 1939. Stand of jovial auctioneers and rendezvous of bargain hunters, it was the scene of many "finds." A violin bought there for threepence is said to have been resold for £300. It is also claimed that the casket containing the freedom of the City of Manchester, conferred on Mrs. Rylands, foundress of the Rylands Library, was discovered on one of the stalls and resold to the city authorities. The curious name of the market is believed to spring from the shape of the plot of land on which it stood.

n right, top : Mr. Charles Clark, the Manchester
ntique dealer, doubtless found a few treasures as
d the visitors to the bookstalls. Mrs. Besley, on
right of lower picture, kept a stall for 40 years
Below : Rylands Library

Slump, Gloom...and the Japs

HOLIDAY makers in the crowded resorts of the Fylde on Whit Monday, 1929, were offered a free spectacle which has never been repeated. The Prime Minister, Mr. Stanley Baldwin, spent that long, sunny day talking politics to them.

From The Mount, Fleetwood, to Blackpool's Palace Theatre and then on to the sands he moved through cheering crowds. With him went Vesta Tilley, otherwise Lady de Frece, wife of the Conservative M.P. for Blackpool. Everywhere they were met with cries of " Good old Vesta ! " and " Baldwin Again ! "

Ten days later Britain, which had been enjoying 18 months of relative prosperity, went to the polls and rejected the Baldwinian slogan of " Safety First."

LOOKING back, we may wonder what safety devices could have insulated Britain entirely from the storm which broke with the Wall Street crash the following autumn. U.S. citizens lost 50 billion dollars, 13,000 banks broke, and the Great Slump followed. It sent down into political defeat both Mr. Baldwin's opposite number in Washington —Mr. Herbert Hoover—and the Socialist Party in Britain.

World trade shrank by 65 per cent and, in Britain, unemployment soared in 18 months from 1,500,000 to 2,700,000. Its peak was reached in the winter of 1932-33 when almost 3,000,000 people were out of work. In the North-West nearly one insured worker in three was on the dole. Coal production was lower than for 30 years and engineering slumped. The suburbs were filled with a new kind of pedlar—the " door-to-door salesman "—and, to keep their idle vessels from rotting in dock, the shipping lines invented cheap cruising for such people as could afford a holiday at all.

THE Great Slump began to recede in the summer of 1933, but one industry remained deeply depressed. There had been a fleeting recovery in the cotton trade in 1925, but by the early 1930's prices faded to the lowest since the Cotton Famine of 1861-65. Wages tumbled down, unemployment in the mills rose to 45 per cent, and, to make matters worse, there was a long cotton-trade lock-out in 1931 followed in 1932 by a damaging strike against attempts to introduce eight looms per weaver in place of the traditional four.

The truth was that over and above the general slump, Lancashire was suffering from a second disease. In spite of the slump, Japan doubled the number of her spindles and looms in six years ; stepped up her exports of cloth to 2,000 million square yards ; drew level with Lancashire and threatened to drive her out of her Eastern markets, especially India.

The moral of this deadly competition was drawn in an article in the EVENING CHRONICLE for April 28th, 1933. It said :

Japan is going up and we are going down. She produces yarn and cloth at lower prices than we can. Her industry's control is more concentrated and profitable. Its mass of workers have to be content with low wages, live in wooden dormitories, mainly on rice and fish, and don themselves in cheap clothing. Japan will throw us back still further unless we change our old-fashioned methods.

This article inaugurated a great debate in Lancashire, but operatives and many employers accepted the moral grudgingly, and Japanese competition continued to be a menace down to the time of the Second World War.

ONE thing the slump did accomplish. It led to an overhaul of mill finances, which has continued to the present time, and to the creation of powerful combinations, including the Lancashire Cotton Corporation, which swallowed 120 spinning mills, saving many from extinction.

THE GREAT SLUMP
Police, mounted and otherwise, clearing the streets of demonstrators
during a disturbance in a Lancashire cotton mill strike in 1932

Rambling is not what it used to be. One used to dress for it—like dressing or dinner—you see there was almost sure to be a photographer around. There was one at Helsby when the above picture was taken. Nowadays it is a much more organized affair, with a " uniform " that is a cross between the dress of a mountaineer and a coalman in spite of the seemingly ubiquitous cameraman. There was one at Lose Hill, Derbyshire, when Mr. G. H. B. Ward, famous Sheffield rambler, handed over the deeds of the Hill to the National Trust in 1945

The Home of Soccer

By IVAN SHARPE

Meredith wins the toss.

An enthusiast

PLAY UP BOLTON

The Presentation Ceremony

Hillman stops a stinger from Taylor.

FIFTY years of Association football in the Red Rose area is a story of honours every year.

Great teams, stars, games, legislators, referees, commentators—it's one long recital of leadership, achievement and triumph.

Take the glamour game—the F.A. Cup. As I write, there have been since 1897 40 Finals. Lancashire has won 13 and lost 8, and also staged 4 replays. Lancashire clubs have thus been represented 21 times—and Burnley have got through to Wembley this year.

Four times in this period the Red Rose has had the Final all to itself.

NOW THE LEAGUE : Lancashire has won the First Division 14 times and the Second Division Championship 13 times in this period. Forty seasons of play, forty Cup and League honours.

But that isn't all. Lancashire and Cheshire have four times lifted the Third Division North Championship in its 18 seasons.

The only time Manchester United have won the Cup in 50 years. It was in 1909 when United boasted a famous half-back line including Charles Roberts (holding cup), Duckworth and Alec Bell

Meredith captained Manchester City in the first All-Lancashire Cup Final, in 1904, when they beat Bolton Wanderers 1—0

No, that's only the start of the story. The League has found all its presidents since 1894 in Lancashire—J. J. Bentley, John McKenna, Charles E. Sutcliffe, and now W. C. Cuff.

Since 1901 its secretaries have been

1 & 2. The first Cup Final at Wembley in 1923 when Bolton Wanderers beat West Ham. The crowd of over 150,000 broke loose and mounted police had to clear the pitch. The match started 45 minutes late. Facing the camera in No. I are R. Pym and David Jack.

3. Dean (Everton) with Toseland in attendance when Everton beat Manchester City in 1933.

4. An aerial view of the great stadium.

5. Manchester City winning the Cup in 1934 when they beat Portsmouth. The referee is S. F. Rous who became Secretary of the F.A.

6. Jack Taylor and Sandy Young of Everton, English Cup winners in 1906.

7. Billy Meredith, the "Welsh Wizard," Manchester United and Manchester City, holder of 51 Welsh Caps, watching the toss at match in 1912.

Tom Charnley and, now, his son-in-law, Fred Howarth, both of Preston, which rightly houses the League's headquarters.

RECORDS? Bolton Wanderers figured in the record English attendance—at the first Wembley Cup Final (" Invasion Day "); were first to score and win the Cup there. They provided the first £10,000 footballer—David Jack. Unhappily, last year also brought to their ground football's worst disaster.

Bury hold the record Cup Final score (6-0 in 1903); Manchester City the greatest provincial gate in England (84,569 in 1934). Everton cherish " Dixie " Dean's record 60 League goals in a season (1927-28) and a feat like winning the Second Division, First Division and F.A. Cup in successive years (1931-2-3).

Burnley claim the longest League run without defeat—30 matches in 1920-21—and now are on the warpath again. And Stockport chip in with the longest match—203 minutes in the Third North Cup-tie with Doncaster in 1946.

PLAYERS? Most appearances for their country in the International Championship stand to the name of Bob Crompton (Blackburn Rovers and England), Elisha Scott (Liverpool and Ireland) and Billy Meredith (Manchester United, City and Wales). Crompton was Lancashire-born; the others made their name here—call them Lancashire by adoption.

Stars galore there have been: Manchester United's famous Duckworth, Roberts, and Bell half-back line, and Burnley's Halley, Boyle and Watson; Bolton's Smith and Vizard, and Manchester City's Tilson and Brook on the wing; plus the most versatile star of all time, Jimmy Crabtree (Burnley), and to-day's England goalkeeper, Frank Swift, who will stand comparison with any rival.

And this is only a quick selection of stars.

REFEREES? John Lewis and T. P. Campbell (Blackburn), J. T. Howcroft and A. E. Fogg (Bolton), H. H. Taylor (Altrincham), L. N. Fletcher (Bury), F. Kirkham and W. F. Bunnell (Preston) come to mind, plus the present party. Accepted experts.

COMMENTATORS? Who did more for football than James Catton, "Tityrus" of the *Athletic News* in Withy Grove? Who saw the game round here grow up? Bob Gowanlock, " Volant " of the EVENING CHRONICLE.

Boastful this may sound. But I can speak so because I'm from the parts the North showed how to play— I'm from London way.

" The heart of Association football is at Manchester Victoria Station on Saturday noon and night," it was once declared. Not far wrong.

THE CONSPIRATORS; OR THE GUY FAWKES OF THE FOOTBALL CHAMBER.

[The Football Association and the Football League, who are to meet in Conference shortly on the subject of players' wages and bonuses, are promised a bombshell from the Players' Union.

The Players' Union, thought by some to be a new movement, was the subject of this *Evening Chronicle* cartoon in 1908

THE HALLE ORCHESTRA, described by Mr. Bernard Shaw as Manchester's chief contribution to the cultural life of England, giving a concert at the old Free Trade Hall in the early 1930's. Sir Hamilton Harty (*inset : close-up*) is conducting. Sir Thomas Beecham (*bottom inset*) was main conductor during the 1914-18 war and again in the mid-Thirties

The Uneasy Thirties

THE 1930's, cradled in slump and buried in war, were less gay, less witty than either the 1920's or the 1900's. This was due partly to normal reaction against the tastes of the previous decade but still more to the long rumblings of approaching battle.

Apart from yo-yo there were few successors of the passing crazes of the Twenties. Their place was taken first by sweepstakes and then by football pools. Streamlining, both where it was suitable and where it was not, was the vogue ; Blackshirts shouted, Belisha beacons were a joke, and the roads were jammed with traffic which mounted at the rate of 500 new cars a day. "Mammoth" became a term of commendation among the uncritical, and so, for a time, did "all-talking-all-singing-all-dancing." Formal manners improved slightly ; speech threatened to grow

dismally stereotyped and, as a reaction against the intellectualism of the Twenties, there was an odd cult of lowbrowism among supposedly well-educated people.

THIS pose, besides being pleasant for genuine numbskulls, had its literary repercussions. Happily they had little effect on books written by Northerners.

Cheshire-born Christopher Isherwood continued the 1920's tradition in "Goodbye to Berlin," while Walter Greenwood's "Love on the Dole" was for its time, what "Hindle Wakes" had been to pre-1914 England. Howard Spring, a Cardiff man, who had laid up much literary raw material in Lancashire became a best seller and James Hilton, born at Leigh, won immense success with novels of dream fulfilment and sentiment.

Other Northern writers claiming notice included Dorothy Whipple, Beatrice Tunstall, Frank Tilsley and John Brophy. Connoisseurs also began to appreciate the fidelity with which Constance Holme had depicted in prose the people of the Lancashire-Westmorland border and the original vividness of L. S. Lowry's paintings of the mean streets.

MUSIC suffered heavily in the slump, but began to recover about 1934. Sir Hamilton Harty left the Hallé amid controversy, but music lovers were consoled by the brilliance and wit of Sir Thomas Beecham, who now spent more time in his native county than for 20 years. Opera did not revive ; its place was taken by ballet, to which Middleton contributed one outstanding dancer—Harold Turner.

Except for Dodie Smith, born and bred at Eccles, Lancashire, produced no outstanding new dramatist. As against this Manchester, Liverpool and Blackpool were more solidly established than ever as centres for staging world premières of theatrical shows.

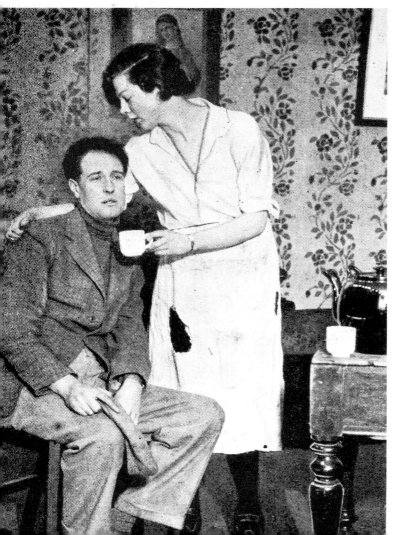

Wendy Hiller, as Sally, and Douglas Quayle, as Larry, i "Love on the Dole" at the Manchester Repertory Theatr

The man who led this fashion was Mr. C. B. Cochran, " one of the few Southerners who really love Manchester." It was a mutual affection. Manchester was kind to him, not only because of his gift for looking and talking like everybody's best uncle, but because he always tried to give Manchester the best one step ahead of London. In 21 years he has put on as many first nights in Lancashire.

It is arguable that his peak was at the end of the Twenties—think of " This Year of Grace," " Bitter Sweet," and the lovely " Wake Up and Dream "—but the Thirties were his busiest decade. He ransacked the world for producers, composers, dancers and actresses to delight audiences at Manchester's Opera House or at the Palace, whose manager, Mr. Jesse Hewitt, had spent a lifetime perfecting his understanding of Lancashire's taste.

Another Lancastrian, George Formby junior, was the most popular young music hall comedian of the Thirties, and radio looked more and more to the North-West for its top-line comedians, led first by Arthur Askey, and later by Tommy Handley and that amalgam of Yorkshire and Lancashire which is Wilfred Pickles.

Enjoyment of these pleasures was heightened by a spell of prosperity from 1935 to 1938. But Lancashire knew it was a narrowly based prosperity, with much unemployment and an ominous drift of workers from the big productive industries. To offset this the North-West tried to develop new industries. In 1936 alone 114 new factories opened in the Manchester region, and but for the war it seems possible that Lancashire would have found, on a new basis, ways to maintain her normal place in the economic life of Britain.

C. B. COCHRAN
AND HIS YOUNG LADIES

The arrival of the company for a new Cochran show was always an occasion. " Cocky " himself always travelled with the cast. In these pictures he is seen with (1) Gertrude Lawrence (on his left), and the Young Ladies. (2) With Ada May. (3) With George Robey and Evelyn Laye when they arrived for " Helen " and, (4) with some of his latest Young Ladies

Above : Miss England II at speed on one of her record runs on Windermere. *Right :* The late Sir Henry Segrave

Scrapbook : 1930-36

"DID WE BREAK THE RECORD ?" These were the first words of the mangled Sir Henry Segrave when he was rescued after the over-turning of his £25,000 speed boat, Miss England II, on Windermere, on June 13th, 1930.

It was already known that he had broken the world record, having covered the first mile at 96.41 m.p.h., and the second at 101.11 m.p.h., when Miss England II struck the water-logged branch of a tree.

Sir Henry suffered terrible injuries and died three hours later. The body of his mechanic, Mr. W. Halliwell, was recovered from the lake next day.

THE ISLE OF MAN was without newspapers for four days and Manchester's burning of gas and electricity exceeded all previous records in the first week of January, 1931,

when England generally, and Lancashire in particular, was blanketed by fog.

The irony of the situation was the business houses had to pay for much of the increased fuel and lighting although the fog which brought land and sea transport almost to a standstill prevented them making any money.

ON JUNE 7TH, 1931, shortly after midnight, shaking houses, rattling windows and falling chimney pots roused thousands of Lancastrians from their beds and sent them running into the streets.

The alarm was caused by the most severe earthquake tremors ever registered in this country. The Fylde and many other parts of Lancashire were shaken for about a minute and the shock was felt over most of the Lake District.

On this occasion the Pendleton Fault, whose movements have caused many minor earth tremors in South Lancashire, could not be blamed. The 'quake, which caused no personal injuries, was more or less general over Europe.

Manchester stepped back three centuries in 1931 when a City Councillor and magistrate (Mr. L. B. Cox) was prosecuted under an Act of Charles II's time for " failing to exercise himself in religious observance on a Sunday."

He pleaded guilty and was duly admonished by the Stipendiary. Mr. Cox argued unavailingly that the law, being out of date, was bad, and that in any event he was but one of 300,000 who had similarly sinned.

The purpose of the prosecution, instituted by the Manchester and Salford Sunday Games League, of which Mr. Cox's brother was secretary, was to call into ridicule ancient Sunday regulations which had not been repealed.

"I shall treasure this visit among the most pleasant memories of my life." The speaker was a little, be-spectacled man, clad

Harking Back : Clothes and vehicles have changed a lot since those days. It would be hard to find such a magnificent wagonette as that in which Manchester United made their triumphal ride from Central Station to the Town Hall when they brought home the Cup in 1909

Mahatma Gandhi with Cotton mill workers during his visit to Lancashire

Sunny Lowry at the time of her Channel swim, from Gris-Nez to St. Margaret's, August 29, 1933. At her first attempt, in 1932, she came within a mile and a half of success

W. H. Dean, another Hyde Seal international. English water polo captain 1911 and 1920. Olympic Games, 1920

in a loin cloth and turning a spinning wheel. He was Mr. Gandhi who, during his visit to Britain for the India Round Table Conference in 1931, made a trip to Lancashire to have "a face-to-face and heart-to-heart talk with cotton workers."

He was cheered by operatives and plied with questions by cotton trade leaders as he sat on the floor of a private house near Darwen turning his wheel, the symbol of industry in the home, which he advocated even though it was directly opposed to Lancashire's interests.

A PLAGUE OF JELLY FISH spoiled the chances of Miss Sunny Lowry, of Levenshulme, breaking a world record when she swam the Channel in 15 hours 45 minutes in August, 1933.

"The jelly fish are making love to me," she called out during the crossing. But for the jelly fish and the cross currents she might have beaten Gertrude Ederle's fastest time of 14 hours 39 minutes.

"YOU WILL BE NO USE IN RUSSIA or England. Perhaps you will be used as manure for our Socialist fields."

Andrei Vishinsky, well-known later for his bouts with Ernest Bevin at U.N.O., has

WORLD BEATERS. The famous Hyde Seal water polo team at their zenith in 1904 when they won every possible cup and trophy, from the World's Championship to the South African Memorial Cup

George Wilkinson, of Hyde Seal. Captained the British team that won the world water polo championship

Marjorie Hinton, Old Trafford, world breast-stroke champion, 200 yards. At the age of 11 was youngest competitor Olympic Games, 1928, and took part in each Olympiad in the 1930's

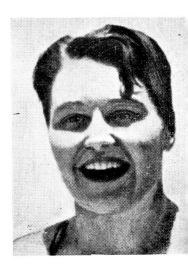

Belle Vue, famous for doing everything in a big way, home of brass band contests, posed this biggest of all massed bands for the Silver Jubilee in 1935

always been a forceful speaker. But when he uttered those threatening words to a Mancunian in 1933, England thought he was carrying forensic vigour too far.

Vishinsky was prosecuting six Metropolitan-Vickers engineers, four of whom had served at Trafford Park, on charges of sabotage, espionage and bribery in the Soviet Union. Three of the accused were sentenced to imprisonment; the rest went free.

Britain, which had always regarded "The Moscow Trial" as political, promptly retaliated with an 80 per cent embargo on Russian imports.

THE PICTURESQUENESS OF MANCHESTER streets lost something when, in 1936, the famous "flying squadron" of "Chronicle Horses" was replaced by motor vans, but the paper and its readers gained considerably by the

YOUR LATE NIGHT FINAL, SIR !

consequent increase in the efficiency of distribution.

Daily these Welsh cobs, slightly taller than polo ponies and specially chosen for their lively action, carried editions of the EVENING CHRONICLE to newsagents, and their departure from Withy Grove was a never-ending attraction for sightseers.

There were about 100 of these "Chronicle Horses" in harness. One of them was the fastest pony in England for his size. He could trot a mile in 2 minutes 17 seconds and keep it up.

IT WAS THE GREATEST BRITISH MINING DISASTER of recent times and nobody knows the cause.

What we do know is that in September 22nd, 1934, there was an explosion at Gresford Colliery, near Wrexham, and that 264 men lost their lives.

Only 11 bodies were recovered; for the remaining 253 the pit is still their grave. It is a consecrated tomb. A week after the explosion the Rev. W. Edwin Jones, Vicar of Gresford, acting on sudden impulse, left morning service at his church, walked in surplice and cassock to the pit head and there quietly read the burial service according to the rites of the Church of England.

The disaster so stirred the public conscience that Relief Funds for the men's dependants realized £567,170.

By the time of the Gresford disaster the use of aircraft for news gathering and photography was a commonplace. These pictures show the Gresford scene and one of the rescue parties

Renaissance

THERE was one year between the wars when, except for the sickness of cotton, the North-West was on top of the world. In 1934 Lancashire were cricket champions, Manchester City won the F.A. Cup, and Stockport-born Fred Perry, master of the forehand-drive, was acknowledged to be the world's finest tennis player.

While Perry was winning the singles championship at Wimbledon, England's eleven were making, at Old Trafford, the biggest cricket score—627—ever piled up against Australia in this country. And a few days later King George V made his last tour of the county to set the royal seal on a series of Lancashire achievements unmatched since the 1890's.

In forty-eight hours he opened Manchester's new Central Library, the great new East Lancashire Road and Queensway, the Mersey road tunnel. All were the fruits of planning in the 1920's. The Library, alongside which a huge extension to Manchester's Town Hall was rising, was the

In Salford presentations were made in Peel Park. The Minister in attendance was Mr. Hore Belisha (on extreme left)

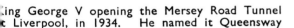

King George V opening the Mersey Road Tunnel at Liverpool, in 1934. He named it Queensway

Lancashire honours for its greatest citizen. *Above :* Lord Derby, with the late Lord Crawford, Chancellor of the University, and Sir John (now Lord) Simon, after receiving an honorary degree at Manchester University in 1931. *Below :* Receiving the Freedom of Manchester from the Lord Mayor (Ald. S. Woollam), 1935

finest built in Britain in a generation. The new arterial road built at a cost of £2,720,000, cut the journey from Liverpool to Manchester by half an hour. The tunnel, most ambitious of its kind in the world, made it possible to go from Liverpool to Birkenhead in six and a half minutes.

In the same year the Vestey brothers gave £220,000 to build a noble tower for Liverpool Cathedral ; Blackburn decided to spend almost as much on a new Cathedral and, a year earlier, the Roman Catholics laid, in Liverpool, the foundations of a cathedral which, in size, will be second only to St. Peter's, Rome.

THE 1930's were altogether a time of big-scale and sometimes imaginative building. The Conservative Government tackled slum clearance energetically ; Manchester began building England's first satellite city at Wythenshawe, and by the end of the decade had erected over 7,000 houses on the estate.

By 1937 Lancashire men could look around and claim that most of their big architectural landmarks—good and bad—had gone up in the previous 40 years. They included semi-skyscrapers like the Ship Canal and Sunlight Houses, or the 322-ft. tall Liver Building, huge hotels like Liverpool's Adelphi and Manchester's Midland (whose acres of terra-cotta were much admired in 1903, but not in 1933), fine new town halls at Lancaster and Stockport, and gigantic hospitals like Manchester Royal Infirmary or Christie's, biggest cancer treating hospital in the Empire.

In many boroughs there had been determined attempts to remove the untidiness left by early industrialism. Rochdale's Town Centre, Bolton's Civic Centre, and Wigan's resolution to rebuild its main streets in the half-timbered style are outstanding examples.

Municipalities were also becoming the heirs of the aristocracy. From 1902, when Burnley bought Townley Hall, hardly a year passed without some famous mansion passing into the care of a town council. The residuary legatee was, usually, the National Trust, which now controls such architectural glories as Speke, Rufford, Lyme and Moreton.

Glorious sunshine and huge crowds greeted King George V on his arrival in Manchester when he toured Lancashire in July, 1934. *Above :* Piccadilly. *Right :* Presenting Silver drums to Manchester Regiment. [Note skeleton of the Midland Bank building in King Street in course of erection, rising above buildings at top left]

WILFRED PICKLES

SHOW BUSINESS

GRACIE FIELDS

(Below)
GEORGE FORMBY

JACK HYLTON
(Back and Front)

FRANK RANDLE

NORMAN EVANS

ARTHUR ASKEY

I. T. M. A.
HANDLEY

T' Northern Union

By WILLIAM MULLIGAN

THE Rugby League game is played by fine athletic men for shrewd, hard-headed, forthright, mainly fair-minded spectators. It is played in Lancashire, Yorkshire and Cumberland, and nowhere else in Britain, but it has roots deep in Australia and New Zealand, and in France it goes from strength to strength.

It is a paradox that it has found favour with the virile people "down under," and with the fiery Latins, but has somehow failed to catch on elsewhere even in such rugby strongholds as South Wales, where professionalism might have been considered not too serious a threat to the existing social order.

No tears are being shed for the sheep that did not come into the fold. Though the old title, "The Northern Union," has gone into limbo, the old savour still clings. There are thousands of supporters who still think of the game only by that name. It is still the custom in many towns to describe somebody or "summat" as "t'best in t'Northern Union."

ONE sometimes wonders what life would be like in Wigan or Widnes, Castleford or Keighley, without the rugby team. Here it is a talking point days before every match; a platform for discussion groups in every pub and club for days after.

No sport commands more loyal supporters; there are few cases on record of conversion from "t'rugby game" to soccer. "It's a mon's game," they say, "and nowt con take that away from it," and, indeed, except in the case of a handful of clubs, one might add: "for players as well as supporters!"

In very few cases do League grounds offer the sumptuous comfort provided by the average Soccer club. To be a real League "fan" calls for hardihood and sacrifice. There is little shelter for the supporters of the so-called "bottom clubs." To them the term "popular side" is a misnomer. It isn't funny to be rained on Saturday after Saturday, but the true-blue Rugby League supporter will stand up to anything. Win or lose, rain or shine, you'll find him standing in his accustomed spot. Rather a pity no one has thought of compiling a spectators' roll of unbroken appearances—there would be thousands on it.

VALENTINE

Wherever it is played the influence of the game has always been for good. It has been good to the old men who have followed a team since boyhood, and to those not so old, and to those who are still very young.

EACH generation has its heroes—a moment's thought brings to mind names like Jimmy Valentine, Jimmy Lomas, Jack Fish, Harold Wagstaff, Billy Batten, Douglas Clark, Billy Hall, Evan Davies, Gwyn Thomas, Jack and Bryn Evans, Alf Ellaby, Johnny Ring, Billo Rees, Jim Sullivan.

In ten years players now popular and admired will be legends like these great names of the past. It won't make the slightest difference to the process if the player runs to 20 stone and keeps a pub. Nobody, least of all a crack rugby player, can suddenly stop being a hero.

THE game has had hard times. A number of clubs were forced to give up during the recent war because their grounds were requisitioned. It was a fight to come back, but not one has fallen by the way. Of the original 22 teams which formed the Northern Union in 1895, 16 are still playing, and only Workington Town of the present league of 28 clubs may be called "juvenile."

THE greatest pride of the Rugby League is its wonderful record in international sport, and we who follow the code have been luckier than most sports followers. We have never had to apologize for being beaten out of hand by an international rival. In test series after test series since 1921 we have held the Ashes against the most vigorous sporting people in the world—the Australians. The "Aussies," great sports that they are, must despair of ever taking the Ashes from us. Rugby League touring teams, up against it, have fought like soldiers defending a redoubt. They have been invincible.

Perhaps because it is exclusively a northern game Rugby League football has never had the credit which we are sure its achievements deserve. Maybe the day will come when its triumphs will be recognized.

Names and Games : 1, James Lomas, England, Salford and Oldham, captain of first Australian tour, 1910 ; 2, Billy Batten, England and Hull ; 3, A. Ellaby, England, St. Helens, Wigan ; 4, Johnny Ring, England and Wigan ; 5, An action scene from the Warrington v. Huddersfield Cup Final at Wembley in 1933 ; 6, Gus Risman, Salford, with Cup, Wembley, 1938 ; 7, Jim Sullivan, Wigan, with R. L. Championship Cup

Swinto

of 1927-28

Broughton Rangers 3-cup team, 1902

It was Best "Left to Joe"

JOACHIM VON RIBBENTROP, Hitler's Foreign Minister, was a noted and prickly socialite during his Ambassadorship in London in the late 1930's.

In 1937 he visited Lancashire and received a check to his notion that the English were effete and unlikely ever to draw the sword against Nazism. When he greeted Manchester's Lord Mayor, " Joe " Toole, with the Brownshirt's salute of the upraised arm, " Joe " pulled down the Ambassador's arm and converted the Nazi symbol into a British handshake.

As this did not deter the ex-champagne traveller from making a long, vehement and typically Nazi speech, Alderman Toole, humorous and downright representative of Lancashire's workers, interrupted the harangue. He told Ribbentrop he had another engagement and marched out of the room.

MILK WAS TWOPENCE A PINT in East Lancashire in 1937. It was the dairies' protest against farmers' refusal to increase the price from 6d. to 7d. as requested by the Milk Marketing Board. E. A. MacDonald, ex-Lancashire and Australian cricketer, was killed in a motoring accident at Blackrod, near Bolton, in July. He was one of the fastest bowlers of all time. Rochdale lost its £136,000 Market Hall by fire in a blaze that could be seen for miles, and Altrincham became a borough. In receiving its Charter it jumped nearly 650 years of history. It was in 1290 that the town received a Court Leet charter from Baron Hamon de Massey, and one of his descendants, the Earl of Stamford, Charter Mayor in 1937, received the new borough charter.

MANCHESTER celebrated the centenary of its incorporation in 1938 and by pageant, exhibition and other spectacular attractions recalled the progress of its municipal enterprise.

An imposing gathering, described by Lord Derby, as " the most representative anyone had ever seen or was likely to see in Manchester," attended a banquet given by Lord Kemsley in honour of the centenary.

Guests included Mr. Lloyd George, Lord Hewart and a long list of Mancunians famous in the arts, commerce and politics. The one exception was Sir John Simon, then Chancellor of the Exchequer, who was born in Yarburgh Street, Alexandra Park, Manchester. He was unable to attend because he was preparing his Budget speech for the following day.

RINGWAY AIRPORT, opened in June, 1938, by Sir Kingsley Wood, was the culmination of a movement began by Sir William Davy during his Lord Mayoralty, 1927-28, which led to the establishment of a small airport at Wythenshawe, making Manchester the first provincial city to have such a scheme. Colonel George Westcott, Lord Mayor, 1928-29, flew back from London with the Air Ministry's licence in his pocket.

Barton Airport, opened in January, 1930, proved unsuitable for modern aircraft, hence Ringway.

A twenty-year-old controversy over the preservation of the old Infirmary site at Manchester's Piccadilly as an open space was settled in 1938 when the scheme for building a new art gallery on the site was dropped.

The art gallery proposal was first put forward in 1910 ; in 1928 a £500 prize was awarded for the best design ; in 1931 the scheme was shelved under a five-year economy plan, and in 1938 it was agreed to leave well alone and allow the citizens to have their City Garden.

While King George VI was touring Royal Ordnance factories in Lancashire on March 31st, 1939, Mr. Chamberlain made his historic statement in the House of Commons that if Polish independence was threatened Britain would at once lend Poland all the support in its power.

The Grand National — The First Fence

A SNOWSTORM RAGED when Grudon won the Grand National in 1901. Many riders objected to the race being run, but the Stewards insisted. The start was a quarter of an hour late

Horses & Men

By CLAUDE HARRISON

IF I had to name a " golden age " of racing —a difficult job seeing that it has been going on in England for centuries—I should probably say it coincided with the first youth of the EVENING CHRONICLE. In the Nineties and Nineteen Hundreds the sport, while remaining " royal," was appealing to the masses. King Edward VII preserved the first aspect and stimulated the second. He loved the turf and was the owner of such splendid horses as Persimmon and Diamond Jubilee, both of whom won the Derby and the St. Leger.

But the great age of racing in the North-West, so far as winning owners and jockeys are concerned, set in after those carefree days had been ended by the war of 1914.

For some years before that date Mr. Edward Hulton was a well known figure in

Below : Steve Donoghue on Captain Cuttle being led in by Lord Woolavington after winning the 1922 Derby

Lord Derby leading in Hyperion after winning the Derby. Tommy Weston is the jockey

the racing world, and in 1916 he won the Derby with a very charming filly, Fifinella, a taking young lady who also won The Oaks. By 1919 he had become Sir Edward Hulton and won the Thousand Guineas with Roseway.

At the same time another Lancastrian flashed across the turf—Jimmy White, of Rochdale, whose vivid and tragic career is dealt with elsewhere in this book. Jimmy never did things by halves, and on the turf he is perhaps best remembered by his gigantic bets and by the parties he gave to his racing and theatrical friends at his Foxhill training quarters. Nevertheless he had, in 1919, one of the best sprinters of the century —Irish Elegance, who won the Salford Borough Handicap at Manchester with 9 st. 9 lb., and the Royal Hunt Cup at Ascot with 9 st. 11 lb. !

THE greatest racing figure who came to the front at this period—and has never receded from that position—was Lord Derby. In 1918 he won the Thousand Guineas with Ferry, and a few years later repeated his success with Tranquil, a filly that also credited him with the St. Leger. Stanley House was reaping the reward of the foundations laid by the late earl, and in 1919

Below : Manchester Cup Day, 1901, the last at the New Barnes course

crowd at the Castle Irwell course

the Doncaster Classic was won by Keysoe in the famous black, white cap.

Lord Derby won his first Derby in 1924. Epsom was a quagmire, fetlock deep, but his colt, Sansovino, won in a canter. His lordship was loudly cheered as he led the horse in, overwhelmed by congratulations. As the jockey dismounted Lord Derby turned to him with a smile and said : " And thank *you*, Tommy." It was also Weston's first Derby success.

Nine years later Weston, once a chainboy with railway horses at Dewsbury, rode his second Derby winner for Lord Derby with that wonderful little horse, Hyperion, the son of Gainsborough.

A FEW years before the start of the First World War a Lancashire jockey was rapidly gaining the favour of the public. I think it was his engaging, self-effacing smile that worked such charm. You will have guessed, of course.

BOTH OLD HANDS. Steve and his favourite mount, Brown Jack, after winning the Ebor Handicap in 1931. Their partnership was famous. Brown Jack made a habit of winning the Queen Alexandra Stakes at Ascot. He did it six times—a record !

Yes, Steve Donoghue, born in a poor street in Warrington.

What a rider he was ! You never saw arms, legs and whips flying. He seemed " of " the horse, not merely on it like a parcel as so many jockeys are. To him reins were silken threads ; no horse ever had a " mouth " through carrying Steve.

Donoghue's record is one of the wonders of the turf. Its crown is six Derby winners, three in successive years. He began his astonishing run on Mr. Solly Joel's Pommern, in 1915, and followed with Mr. Fairlie's Gay Crusader two years later. Then in 1921, 1922 and 1923 he won the race on Mr. J. B. Joel's Humorist, Lord Woolavington's Captain Cuttle, and Mr. Ben Irish's Papyrus. His sixth was Mr. H. Morris's Manna, in 1925. No wonder the cry, " Come on, Steve ! " was known in places far removed from the racecourse.

In the Second World War, Lord Derby again had a long run of racing successes. He won classics with Watling Street (The Derby, 1942), Herringbone (1,000 Guineas and St. Leger, 1943), Garden Path (2,000 Guineas, 1944), and Sun Stream (1,000 Guineas and The Oaks, 1945). All were ridden by Harry Wragg, a native of Sheffield,

at first known as " Sheff." But so adept did he become at riding a waiting race that he earned the nickname of " Head Waiter." This shrewd North country jockey decided to retire at the end of last season—finishing at Manchester with three winners on the last day, including Las Vegas, who carried off the November Handicap.

The war years were also years of victory for Willie Nevett, born of working-class parents at Chorley, and sent as a boy to be apprenticed to Dobson Peacock, at Middleham. Willie has ridden with great success for the stable. Between 1941 and 1945 he rode three Derby winners—Owen Tudor, Ocean Swell, and Dante. And the first two were " chance " mounts rejected by the stable's first jockey !

Who was the most picturesque racing character of the last 50 years ? It was another North-Westerner—Lord Lonsdale. With his topper, cigar and buttonhole he was known to everybody from Stewards of the Jockey Club to gypsies on Epsom Downs. The arrival of his bright yellow car was always the signal for a rush towards it. His one big triumph was when Royal Lancer won the St. Leger in 1922, but no great racing picture was complete without him.

Within a mile of the centre of smoky old Manchester, Castle Irwell presents a country scene on a sunny day

World War II

"In the end the world always has a day of reckoning with men like Hitler," said the EVENING CHRONICLE leading article on September 1st, 1939. Nobody then foresaw that the day would be nearly six years in coming. While bombs rained on Warsaw, 19,000 Manchester schoolchildren, singing "South of the Border," took train for the country. All were safely away by September 3rd when, on a morning of mellow sunshine, Mr. Neville Chamberlain told Britain that for the second time in 25 years, she was at war with Germany.

There is no need to retail for readers in 1947 a detailed narrative of the Second World War. They may have forgotten that petrol was rationed as early as September 23rd, 1939; that the original sugar ration was three-quarters of a pound; meat 1s. 10d. worth for each person, and that when theatres and cinemas were shut in the first days of war consumption of alcohol soared 50 per cent. But the emblems of that first wartime winter are vividly remembered. They were burst sandbags, lost gasmasks, torches, taped windows, and evacuees. Even the evacuees were becoming "untypical" before spring 1940. Of 38,000 who had gone to Cheshire 30,000 had returned home.

Indeed the most determined attack on Britain that winter was made by the weather. Temperatures dropped almost to zero in Manchester, there were ice floes in the Mersey and the death rate jumped to 240 per cent above average. A huge snow imprisoned families for days; road and rail transport was chaotic—and not a word about it appeared in the papers.

The rooted belief that a hard winter breeds a fine summer was justified and, in glorious weather, Hitler conquered Western Europe. A nightingale might sing in Berkeley Square, but there was no more talk of hanging out washing on the Siegfried Line. Instead the North-West was busy uprooting signposts and looking for shotguns to arm the Local Defence Volunteers, created overnight after an appeal by Mr. Anthony Eden. Their

sinews were the middle-aged veterans of the Somme, Ypres and Salonika, but in the next four years, they embraced every imaginable type of recruit. Even the post offices of Lancashire, town hall staffs, and dispersed workers like the colliers formed their own companies and battalions.

"Sireens" sounded in earnest were scarcely heard in the North-West before the days of the Battle of Britain. What the Luftwaffe then did to Lancashire is still written in the willow-herb covered open spaces of Liverpool, Manchester and Salford. Vanished, damaged buildings rise once more in the mind's eye—Liverpool's Customs House and Cathedral Lady Chapel; Manchester's Cathedral; the roof of the great Exchange, Free Trade Hall, Piccadilly "winged with red lightning and impetuous rage." Among the ruins move the figures of heroic firemen and Civil Defence

Yes. We were "in it" again!

This was one of the great secrets of the war . . . censors said that the weather was not to be mentioned. In February, 1940, the whole of the North-West was snow and ice-bound. Here the beach at Morecambe is seen completely covered with ice-floes

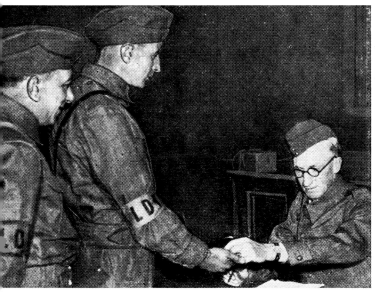

workers, of "clippies" calling everybody "Love," or humming "There'll Always Be An England."

After the summer of 1941 the baffled Luftwaffe retired and troubled the North-West little except for a V-bomb attack during the last Christmas of the war, when many people were killed at Oldham.

It was in Salford, in 1940, that the answer to the V-2 was discovered, well in advance of the menace. Mr. G. M. Tomlin, experimenting at the headquarters of Salford Electrical Industries, detected an electrical reaction he had not foreseen. This was the germ of the proximity fuse, the device which enables a shell to "sense" when it is near enough to a target to do damage and then explode.

Americans reckoned the proximity fuse second in importance only to the atom-bomb, and here, again, it was Lancashire applying the knowledge won by Rutherford, that led the way. Sir James Chadwick, bred and educated in Manchester, was Britain's leading atomic-bomb scientist. Professor J. D. Cockcroft, born on the borders of

The "funny men" called them the Look, Duck, Vanish, but as the Home Guard it was soon a force to be reckoned with

'IS THIS WHERE WE CAME IN?'' Politically, in pictures, anyway; we return to W. S. Churchill—back in Manchester, this time on his great election tour of 1945. As he filled the tiny market place in 1908 so he almost filled the huge Piccadilly square in 1945

Yorkshire and Lancashire, is now head of the nation's atomic research, and the pioneer work of Professor P. M. S. Blackett in atomic physics should not be overlooked, though he disclaimed any close responsibility for the evolution of the bomb.

The history of the North-West's war effort has yet to be written. It is possible to mention only a few of the fruits—the Lancaster Bomber, the Franks Flying Suit, the equipment of the "Frog" men, the development and application of radar.

Our regiments served in every major campaign. The 2nd Battalion of the Lancashire Fusiliers, repeatedly commended by Lord Montgomery, claimed to be the most decorated battalion in the British Army.

They won one V.C., five D.C.M.'s, 23 M.C.'s, 38 M.M.'s, one M.B.E., and 15 Mentions in Dispatches.

At Dunkirk Major Ervine Andrews became the first Army V.C. of the war while serving with the 1st Battalion of the East Lancashires covering the beach defences. There were three battalions of the Cheshires in the evacuation; other battalions went with Wavell to Benghazi and fought at Alamein, through Tunisia and Sicily and on to Italy.

Men of the Manchesters served in 11 countries and three continents. The 1st Battalion were part of the force that fought the doomed rearguard action in Malaya in 1942. They lost half their number in battle, or in Japanese prison camps. Other battalions were at Malta and Iceland, while Caen, Falaise, the Seine, Nijmegen and the Rhine mark their track in the great invasion which, in May, 1945, brought at last the day of reckoning with Hitler and with Nazidom.

PROUD PARENTS
" Yes, old chap . . . born this morning."

Lee

" Have you seen Lee ? " This has been a nightly remark in Northern homes for nearly 12 years. It was on November 18th, 1935, that Evening Chronicle readers began " Laughing with Lee." Since then he has contributed over 3,000 drawings to the paper.

Lee—Joe to his friends—is a 45-years-old Yorkshireman and, when he is " in the mood," it takes him about three hours to think of a cartoon and complete it.

He excels as the kindly satirist of suburbia. The setting of his first Evening Chronicle cartoons was a narrow garden, fenced chin-high and enfolding a fish pond behind a semi-detached house with sham Tudor gabling. No one has ever hit off such homes so neatly. Joe Lee has always preferred to live among them himself.

New Blood in The Hallé

The most problematical phase in the history of Manchester's Hallé Concerts since their founder raised his baton to conduct his first concert in 1858 was in 1943.

During four wartime seasons the orchestra deprived of its traditional home, the Free Trade Hall, gave concerts in theatres and cinemas, mostly under the conductorship of Dr. Malcolm Sargent. Then the Hallé Society boldly decided to change its policy, turning the orchestra from a part-time organization to a full-time body giving 200 concerts a year. John Barbirolli was brought from America to be permanent conductor, but the orchestra offered him was largely young and inexperienced—the B.B.C. had bid successfully for most of the " old " Hallé's leading players. The question was : Could the new orchestra hope to bear comparison with the old ?

Barbirolli rehearsed his musicians for weeks, made his debut at Bradford on July 5th, 1943, and in the next six months gave 126 concerts to 250,000 listeners in 34 cities. By this time the new Hallé was firmly launched, immensely popular and an artistic success.

An amusing discord sounded a year later when Sir Thomas Beecham returned from wartime residence in U.S.A. The Hallé held that his presidency of the Society had lapsed in his absence. Sir Thomas, never the man to take deposition lying down, retorted tartly that he had not resigned and would not resign.

A wordy, witty battle, over which all England grinned, followed. The verbal honours went to Sir Thomas. " Barred " from the Hallé, he went to his native Merseyside and, amidst acclamation, appeared as guest conductor with the Liverpool Philharmonic Orchestra, which during the war years, had scrapped its dependence on the Hallé and built up a fine body of musicians with the best concert hall in Britain.

Whitsuntide Walks, a Lancashire institution for a century and a half, have always been the barometer of current fashion. The grown-up-looking girls in this procession at Weaste in the 1900's were only sixteen or seventeen years old

A Manchester Whit-Monday Walk in the late 1930's. Children with banners are seen at the junction of Deansgate and Victoria Street. In the background is the Victoria Hotel

Not all Cotton . . .

By Louis Golding

WE are both taking stock, the EVENING CHRONICLE and I. The EVENING CHRONICLE is fifty years old, and I am about a year older. We were both quite young when Queen Victoria died, but the occasion combined my first experience of impersonal grief and of contemporary journalism.

They brought in a copy of the EVENING CHRONICLE and its front page was framed in thick black margins. I have seen the funereal judas-tree in purple flower, and the catafalque of a dead bishop, but nothing ever struck me as so solemn and so tragic as the black-margined page of the EVENING CHRONICLE that day.

THEY talked in whispers of the dead Majesty. Though not by birth a Jewish lady, I gathered from the grief-stricken family she had a "Jewish heart," which was to be inherited some years later by a Gentile closer to me, the late John Lewis Paton, my High Master at the Manchester Grammar School.

There in the iron-barred kitchen of our house, Ten Harris Street, in Strangeways, I contemplated the image of the defunct Queen, who was Empress, also, of India, and potentate over many powers and principalities. I hid my face in the EVENING CHRONICLE, but my grief was too much for me. Suddenly I started howling at the top of my voice.

OFTEN and often in the years to come I was to return in my writings to that iron-barred kitchen in Harris Street ("Angel Street" I called it), and to Howard Street, also in Strangeways, where my mother died and the EVENING CHRONICLE published an edition of the paper with black margins, one copy only,

for circulation exclusively in my own heart. And to Sycamore Street, up in Hightown, which (in case it might interest the reader) was the original "Magnolia Street," if there *was* one single original street, with the Jews living in the odd-numbered houses, and the Gentiles in the even.

The horizon, you see, was widening. I had gone up the hill to Hightown. I had gone beyond the railway bridge to be a Scholarship boy at Manchester Grammar School. I went out upon exciting adventures in Lancashire and Cheshire. Since then then I have travelled further afield, far, far from Manchester.

BUT how right Mr. Julian Symons is, in a recent essay by him devoted to "The Manchester School"! (He means the novelists, not the economists):

"It is clear that the Manchester background is important to these writers, as it is to the characters in their books. They are always coming back to it."

Quite true, certainly as far as I am concerned. Always coming back to it.

And yet how many years was it that I actually lived in Manchester? The first eighteen of my half-century. Then came Oxford, London, Paris, Athens, New York, Berlin, to mention some major towns, and ten thousand villages, encampments, oases. But always, if not in the flesh, then in the spirit, back to Manchester, Lancashire, Cheshire, back to the home pastures.

Why? Because in the early years experience does not merely slide over surfaces, it burns into texture. After all, they are *new* things you are seeing, hearing, feeling. You have rarely or never, seen, heard, felt them before. A tram passes by you at night, clanging along the cobbles of Bury New Road. For the first time you become aware of the mystery of people brought momentarily into your orbit of experience, and swept ineluctably away. Who *are* they—no: who *were* they? Whither going? Why? A common speculation, you will say. But oh, what thrilling thoughts, the the first time you think them.

Or walking along the Irwell a vast distance beyond Agecroft Bridge, or vast it seemed, suddenly I was in " country." There was a coppice crammed as thick with bluebells as the knitting in a scarf. How I sang! How I waved my cap in the air! (It was not even a Manchester Grammar School cap yet.) I have since seen acres upon acres of scarlet anemones compact under Delphi, a golden-yellow convolvulus overspreading like a turgid flood, a high plateau in Yosemite. I think the general landscape, there in Greece, and there in California, was as superb as any this planet holds. But I was older. My hat stayed on my head.

Well, I will go back to those eighteen years, each of which was longer than all my other years put together. I will extract from them a moment here, a person there, as the iron compulsion of caprice dictates.

Manchester. Well, of course, first there was home, and then there was school. Home was at its most beautiful with the brass trays, the brass candlesticks, the brass samovar, which my mother cherished only less devotedly than us, her children. And there was the extraordinary molten silver

JOHN LEWIS PATON, M.A., High Master
Manchester Grammar School, 1903-24

of my father's voice, which he used with subtle virtuosity when he made orations at the synagogue on high days and holidays.

And school was the Elementary School; first Waterloo Road, and then Southall Street. Waterloo Road, alas, I chiefly recall, because teacher strangled a rabbit in a straw basket for that week's ration of nature-study. I was too wretched even to put my hand up and ask could I be sick, please, which would have been helpful. On the other hand, I remember Miss Brown of Standard Six, very tall and gaunt, with steel-framed spectacles. She loved me, I was to realize years later, at an age when unrequited love was usually the other way round. But she wore corsets that clanked like the galvanized buckets her father sold in his Shudehill ironmongery shop. Southall Street was more blissful, because Mr. Ashworth took Standard Six, and Mr. Bradburn took Standard Seven, and they talked about things like the Rings of Saturn and the Apples of the Hesperides.

Then, of course, school was the Manchester Grammar School. I think that from the beginning that largely meant J.L.P. for me. Those blue eyes, like pebbles washed in glacier water. That piece of string sticking

B[
Sa
di
Ce
Ro
to
Ri
Le
wi
an
at

er and
 Picca-
 Place.
Street,
d Vic-
ground.
hedral.
 King
rsonnel
e team
ospital

out from a rear pocket. Those arms bared to the sleeves, over the galley at school camps. The kindness, the purity, the valour. Those were J.L.P. That was the sort of school he sought to make of it. And did not fail.

WHAT, then, of Manchester writers and writing during those early years ? I did not know in the flesh any of the majors, C. E. Montague, Allan Monkhouse, Stanley Houghton. However, later in London, I was to meet the genial Harold Brighouse, and to tell him of my admiration for his cotton novel, *Heppenstalls*, and to bemoan the crassness of publishers who do not rush the masterpiece into print and keep it there. And James Agate I was to meet in London often—as who can fail who is at all active in the London scene ? The first time I recall well, in the *Saturday Review* office of Filson Young, also a Lancashire writer. It was the very early Twenties, both of us beginning our metropolitan writing careers, he as dramatic critic, I as reviewer and writer of " middles." The last time I recall well, too. We were flanking Mr. Rank at a film luncheon. The white arcs glared and sizzled, the cameras turned and moaned. It seemed to me " James " was as talented a film star as a writer.

BUT I am digressing from Manchester, and the eighteen years. What of writers at school, nearer my age ? Those who might have been

best went to that first war, and did not come back again. But there was L. du G. Peach, to achieve fame on the air. I recall him only as a meritorious Falstaff in Mr. Garnett's annual play, in the Lecture Hall.

Harold Laski I see vividly doffing his braided prefect's cap and putting on a top hat and striped grey trousers to attend a political meeting at the Labour Hall in Strangeways. One might have thought that it was the bluest section of the Tory Party he was to adorn in days to come.

But most important in my own development was the little writer's group that " Tommie " Moult assembled round him in his house in Sedgley Park. I was fifteen and read poems that sounded like it. " Tommie " was writing his first novel, " Snow Over Elden," from which he read the chapter about the cold bath. We neither asked for mercy, nor gave it.

What grim surgeons of letters we were !

So much for Manchester in those first years.

CHESHIRE ? I recall my first wanderings along Mersey banks. And a kingfisher, positively a kingfisher ! And how I visited Chester for the first time, and they pointed out a smooth dingy-grey wall and said the Romans had built it. And I recall the tense, antiquarian emotion with which I went up to the wall and kissed it. And I have never felt deceived or undeceived about that episode, though I now know the wall would be 1902

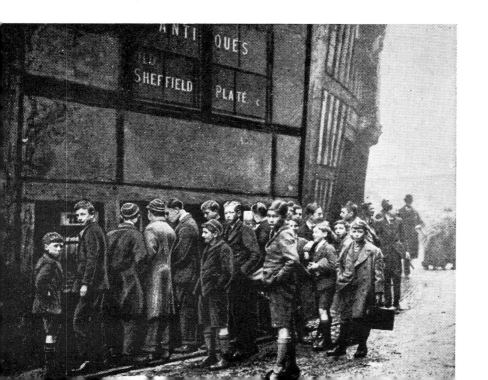

The M.G.S. tuckshop was on the Poets' Corner in Long Millgate

or thereabouts. It was the classical world I was embracing—and was not to feel more moved, later, in the tomb of Menelaus in the Peloponnese.

Lancashire. How little of cotton or the cotton towns was in my Lancashire! There was a first glimpse of the sea at Southport—most exciting, though far off. And there were the green slopes of Southern Windermere, the meadowsweet by the stream, the bracken uncurling, the gallant spires of foxglove . . . all, all faint in the mist of Lancashire " high tea."

Ah, " high tea " ! Ah, boyhood memories of the bells tolling down the darkling distances, while before me, behind me, the teaspoons clink with sweet music in the " high tea " cups ! Hot batch-cakes, heavily buttered, slices of " coorant bread," brawn, collared bread, celery, cakes—called of Eccles, called of Simnel—this jam and that, apple tart with cheese . . all washed down with deep draughts of strong tea or deeper draughts of stronger barley wine.

A cup of tea in one hand, a glass of barley wine in the other, I raise a jubilee toast to friends dead and living, and " high teas " long ago.

The Greatest Lancastrian

"Britain's Best Recruiter." This was the name given Lord Derby during the First World War, and the description holds good to this day.

It was Lord Derby who suggested the formation of the " Pals " Battalions, but he is best remembered as author of " The Derby Scheme," introduced in 1915, when he was Director-General of Recruiting.

Under it men attested and were grouped. By the end of the year 2,000,000 had attested and of these 830,000 were available for service after deducting the men in reserved occupations.

The scheme had its critics, mainly because so many young men remained in sheltered jobs. But this was the fault of the Civil Departments, not of Lord Derby. His own criticism of the scheme was that it was late in the field and should have been launched before the war.

Lord Derby's aim was to preserve the voluntary system, and in this he so far succeeded that conscription was staved off until 1916. Thereafter he became Minister of War before going to Paris as the most popular Ambassador in living memory.

Lancashire's biggest birthday greeting was sent in April, 1935, when Lord Derby celebrated his 70th birthday. Over 83,000 people signed the message which recalled with gratitude " the largeness of sympathy and the generosity of spirit which have made your Lordship welcome in every assembly and endeared you to the hearts of Lancashire people."

The signatures filled 22 volumes and were accompanied by the gift of a gold rose water dish and jewel for Lady Derby. To comply with Lord Derby's wish that the presentation should not compete with charitable appeals before the public, subscriptions were limited to a shilling a head.

Although still incomplete, Liverpool Cathedral dominates the city. The great tower, erected through the munificence of the Vestey brothers, is almost finished. In the foreground are the blitzed shells of Liverpool's business quarter. On the right is the drum which supported the dome of the gutted Customs House

My Lancashire

By the Rt. Hon. Lord Woolton

LANCASHIRE to me means home ; it means the home of people of direct speech, deeply rooted principles and loyalties. The pride of Lancashire men in the county of their birth is known wherever the English language is spoken. It is a peculiar pride. There are, of course, among people less fortunately born, those who think that whatever reasons for pride there may be in being born in this wet and smoky county have long since created an unlovely spirit of arrogance. But it is a pride that is based on generations of accomplishment.

For what should we look in the history of a county ? For good fellowship, for men of high principle, for leaders in public affairs, for wide culture of citizenship of the world, for commercial enterprise and scientific attainment ; for good sportsmanship and for all or some of these to be found among people living amidst natural beauty. There is a catalogue of attributes that might make any other county in the country declare that this was too much to ask, and yet Lancashire can respond to any of them.

FIRST let me deal with natural beauty, for that will be the first shock to the foreigner. The Southerner thinks of Lancashire in terms of wet and smoky Manchester. Of course it rains in Manchester, but in what part of England can one find scenery to beat the view from Pendle Hill ? The inhabitants of Westmorland who go to live on Lake Windermere for its beauty, are finding that comfort in the views of the opposite shore on the soil of Lancashire ; and beyond lies all the gorgeous scenery of Coniston, mountain and lake.

I have taken up the challenge on natural beauty because that was the point at which we might have been judged most vulnerable. To the rest of the challenge we can go forth with easy confidence.

Men of principle—yes, indeed, we breed them men of stubborn principle, unyielding in the maintenance of what they conceived to be right. Chartists, in their demand for political freedom ; Nonconformity in defiance of the Church ; Catholics in the preservation of their belief ; Suffragettes in rebellion against masculine tyranny—all these movements are a part of the history of Lancashire. Men of vision, too, were our forefathers—Hugh Oldham, Bishop of Exeter, who so long ago as 1515 saw the advantage to England of educating the boys of his native north and founded a charity school for the purpose—the Manchester Grammar School.

MANY benevolent men and women of the middle period in our history founded charitable institutions for education. Therein lies the origin of most of our public schools, which, for the most part, have forgotten the purpose of their foundation—or maybe conditions have altered the need. But Manchester has not forgotten, and whilst happily the changed conditions of society no longer makes Hugh Oldham's words appropriate to the new entrants to this school, it remains to this day a school into which boys can come without regard to their parents' capacity to pay. And how magnificently has it fulfilled Hugh Oldham's dream ! It stands supreme among the day schools of Great Britain. "Eton and Manchester," a great Minister of Education, Mr. R. A. Butler, told me one day, " are the great schools of England." I agreed with him ; politeness demanded it, for he was educated at one of them and I at the other.

One should note in passing that it was in the year after Hugh Oldham founded the Manchester Grammar School that Collet founded St. Paul's School in London. I agree that there are other schools in Lancashire, some of them public schools that have produced good men of affairs and great athletes; secondary schools, mechanics institutes, technical schools that have added a wealth of knowledge to this country—but when I am asked what Lancashire means to me, my mind turns with affectionate gratitude to this ancient foundation whose pupils have enriched England with their knowledge and by their competence have moulded much of its administration.

From such thoughts one goes on to the university—the greatest of the modern universities and the progenitor of several. John Owens, unhappily for him crossed in love, fortunately for England, remained a bachelor and left his fortune to found a college. It differed from Oxford or Cambridge in too many ways to describe. One of its differences made its future greatness. It recognized no religious bar; its professors were free from any religious test. Here, in this vital and prosperous city where men already had won reputation for commercial enterprise, was opportunity for freedom for the learned. Hence it was that Alexander, a Jew, came to Manchester to become one of the leading philosophers of the world. Perkin, who first opened up the fields of organic chemistry, did his researches here. Schuster, again a Jew, whose brilliant work founded the University's physical laboratories in which afterwards

Rutherford became famous, and in which Sir James Chadwick did his early work in the discovery of atomic energy, settled here.

From this university—then called the Victoria University—there separated the University of Liverpool, which arose from the foundation under the impetus of pious and learned and public-spirited Unitarians of the Liverpool College; and subsequently the universities of Leeds and Sheffield. Tens of thousands of Lancashire men and women owe their happiness and their living—and, maybe in rarer cases, the foundations of their fortunes; to the fact that they were the pupils of these outstanding men who sought freedom for religious faith amidst their academic teaching in the foundation of John Owens.

The name brings to my mind the other Owen, Robert, dreamer and economist, who had a modern belief in the wide extension of capitalism and so created the Co-operative movement, which has grown to such enormous dimensions. And though it is a smaller and less momentous thing there is that other co-operative movement that has nothing to do with business, the Co-operative Holidays Association, which arose in Lancashire in the vision and enterprise of a young Congregational parson, T. Arthur Leonard. He saw a better way for the young men and women of his congregation to spend their holidays than on the crowded beaches of popular resorts, and took them on long walking tours amidst the beauty spots of England and Scotland. So arose a movement, which brings companionship, and health and joy to succeeding generations of the young.

All these things are Lancashire to me, and they are great things; and the nation inherits them. Alongside of them surely we must give almost equal place to the commercial enterprise of Lancashire men. Hard bargainers these, but firm in their faith. I know no sight more creditable to Lancashire commerce than that—now, alas, sacrificed in a new-planned world—of the Liverpool Cotton Exchange on a busy day. There immense transactions took place with no more than a nod of the head or a raising of the hand. At the end of the day when the

Until 1921 the North boasted two great towers, the New Brighton Tower was even higher than that at Blackpool, 625 feet compared with 520 feet

records were compiled it was almost unknown for anyone to have gone back on their bargain. Their word was as good as their bond. And herein lay the genius of another great Lancashire project, now a world-wide institution, The Royal and Liverpool, London and Globe Insurance Companies.

Liverpool men founded these bodies; they remain domiciled in Liverpool with branches all over the world. But when the San Francisco disaster took place and insurance was badly hit, the Liverpool men put their private fortunes behind these companies to enable them to meet their bonds. British financial integrity was involved; and Lancashire men knew only one way to deal with that situation—to pay in full. British insurance owes debt to those men of Lancashire for that act. They were commercial statesmen and fine gentlemen. Their descendants have maintained their traditions, and not only Lancashire, but the whole Empire, benefited. In public affairs this county has made its contribution to national life—and indeed to history. It has produced men who have occupied the world stage with distinction—Gladstone, Cobden and Bright, Morley. Surely the Free Trade Hall should be rebuilt, if only as a memorial to the statesmen Lancashire has produced and as a proper world platform for the statesmen of the future.

IF I ended my reflections on such a note I should have left out a scene of combat beloved by all Lancashire men, Old Trafford, known where cricket is played the world over as a field of sportsmanship, as the arena of high struggle and tough fighting in Britain's most glorious game. What Lancashire man has not known the joy of playing at hate as he has watched Yorkshire playing at Old Trafford on a Bank holiday? I could not think of Lancashire without thinking of its cricket or without a feeling of gratitude that I have enjoyed the privilege of friendship with the President of the Lancashire Cricket Club, Lord Derby, surely the embodiment of everything that is excellent in Lancashire life and character.

These are the things that Lancashire means to me, and they are vital, invigorating and proud things; for it is a great County.

During these Fifty Great Years millions of holiday-makers have basked in the shadow of Blackpool's Tower

CURRENTLY AVAILABLE IN THE REPRINT SERIES
by
'Memories'

£4.95

Cricket
by
SILAS K. HOCKING

A TALE OF HUMBLE LIFE

Her Benny
by
SILAS K. HOCKING

THE ORIGINAL ILLUSTRATED EDITION

CHIPS
by
SILAS K. HOCKING

THE ORIGINAL ILLUSTRATED EDITION

£3.95

£4.95

Also available by *'Memories'* . . .

THE HISTORY OF . . .

MANCHESTER BUSES
by Ted Gray - £3.50

MANCHESTER TRAMS
by Ted Gray - £3.50

SALFORD DOCKS
by Cliff Hayes - £2.95

for full list of books available, please write to:-
NORTHERN PUBLISHING SERVICES
28 BEDFORD ROAD, FIRSWOOD
MANCHESTER, M16 0JA